1st OFFENSE

THE BEGINNING
OF THE END

1st OFFENSE

THE BEGINNING
OF THE END

BRIAN HARPER

EMAJINAYARTS

EMAJINAYARTS PUBLISHING, LLC

WEST BLOOMFIELD, MI

EMAJINAYARTS

EMAJINAYARTS PUBLISHING, LLC
WEST BLOOMFIELD, MI

InCogEgo: The Blogs and Journals of an Introverted Soul previously
appeared as blog posts on www.emajinay1stoffense.blogspot.com

FIRST EMAJINAYARTS PUBLISHING PAPERBACK EDITION 2015

ISBN-13: 978-0-692-40181-1
ISBN-10: 0-692-40181-4

LIBRARY OF CONGRESS
2015921149

CONTENTS

To my Dad,

My Zen master. Your quiet wisdom is guiding me through this life, as much as you may not believe it, because I've been a real bonehead, but it's true. When I was a boy you told me I could be an author and an artist, and that these are my gifts. It's taken me some time I know, and I know you were afraid that I'd let it all go to waste, but I assure you I'll always do my best to prevent that. This is for you, thank you for believing in me, I know you always have. I love you.

MAMA

You are my Giving Tree.
I wanna strive and live to
make you proud.
Proud that you gave birth to me.
I'm so proud that God placed you on Earth for Me.
Proud that you endured for me,
9 months of hurt for me.
Thank you Mama for supporting me and adoring me.
Seeing more and more in me,
Absorbing me with every prayer,
You put the Lord in me.

Mama you are to me what
a blanket was to Linus,
A life without You would be equal
to subtraction without the minus.

I love you in ways I cannot explain.

BRIAN HARPER X

To my Jasmyn Love
you are my world, and I love you with all my heart.

BABY LIVE

Baby live.
Baby cherish life.
Enjoy it now.
Know that you've enjoyed ALL
of your yesterdays, and anticipate
Your tomorrows with enthusiasm.
Enjoy today.
Cherish it now.
Enjoy life for always.

For when I see you I see my
Future fleeing and
yours only expanding.
In you I see the
image of my former self,
Simultaneously with the self I
Never became and
dreamed I would become.
I see you and pray that you become
all of that and more. 100 fold.
Be it all.
Be all of the YOU that YOU can be!
Baby live. Child grow.
Seek knowledge for it is power.
Apply knowledge for it will empower YOU.
Be ambitious without any inhibitions
to impede your progress in any way.
Strive.
Strive through this life and through this journey.

No matter how treacherous the path
may seem, no matter the duration;
Endure.
Stumbling blocks may make you stumble
but determination will give you the
strength to step over the next group
of pitfalls you encounter.
You will have the strength to stand strong again.
Stand strong.
Kill doubt with confidence!
Have faith.

Believe.
Believe in yourself; as I believe in you.
Love yourself.
See yourself the way God sees you.
You are special.
You are one of the Creators finest Creations.
His cherished child.
Know that God delights in you.
You are annointed.
Run with your gifts.
Run toward, never AWAY from your dreams!
For life is but a dream,
Don't run from life.
Baby embrace.
Embrace the present.
Be "still" in it.
Let it engulf you.
Listen.
Hear and heed wise council.
Hear your heart, hear God within
and let God guide you.

Apply action to faith,
for faith without works is dead.
Aim high.
You'll go places you
could never fathom.
You'll go places you've
Never dreamed of.
Be happy.
Baby live.
Love.
Learn.
Leave a legacy.
Live in such a manner that will
make the Lord proud.
This world it will be a better place
Simply because you exist in it.
Give this world someone and something;
To remember.
Baby live.

FIELD OF JASMYN'S

The truly natural things in life are dreams,
The one thing nature can't decay,
Jasmyn you live in my dreams,
Therefore my love for you will never fade away,
Of all the things you'll learn in life,
I hope you get that,
I hope you never miss that,
I love you with all my heart n'
I hope you never forget that!
My love for you will remain long after I'm gone,

My love will fly to you on the wings of carrier doves
that replaced pigeons,
The trees will whisper I love you in the breeze.

Flowers will bloom from your tears,
The sun will rise each time you smile,
The meadows are full of your promise,
Creeks and streams flow to deltas
that empty into lakes & oceans
of endless possibilities;
For you.

In this place, in the night time,
Even without sun,
No moon, no stars that shine,
The only light there is, is you.
A place where anyone or anywhere
You wanna be;
You ALREADY are!

Here the stars bow in
obeisance to your commands,
They shine as bright as you demand them to,
and they align themselves in
any formation that you see fit,
Here, you design your own constellations.

You were placed on this Earth,
in this field to be cherished, admired and adored,
to be loved and regarded with reverence,
and to be honored.

This is your field of dreams,

A place where you can resurrect history,
Recreate it, and also create your own.
A field of dreams full of all and as many
dreams that you can possibly dream,
Stretching as far as your eyes can see!
All of your dreams, all of the dreams you've dreamt,
and what dreams may come.

INTRODUCTION

This book has been over ten years in the making. It has been a painstaking journey, a labor of both love and pain. Initially I thought to myself that this will be my own personal catharsis. My own way to heal and mend my brokenness. The thought of publishing my poetry really wasn't at the forefront of my ideas at the beginning, I simply wrote for the sake of it. Writing is a way for me to clear my own air, to *vent*. Only after sharing some of my poems with friends or colleagues from time to time, and through their encouragement, did the idea vaguely enter into my mind. So I continued to write as a catharsis, challenging myself to vent as creatively as I could. But as time moved on and the more I wrote, it began to take the form of something much more.

When I suffered from severe depression, I felt very alone and isolated. I avoided everyone and everything, and had nowhere to turn. *Phone calls to Brooklyn! Phone calls to Brooklyn!* Thank God for the conversations I had with my dear cousin Sonia and the many letters sent back and forth between my Aunt Jackie and I in 2000. My cousin Sonia suggested that I write poetry to vent. At 19, I began. I was expressing emotions that I felt only I alone was experiencing. But over time I realized that I was not alone in my struggles with depression and anxiety, and the struggles of life in general. Depression and anxiety are epidemics in our society. My perspective changed in light of this truth. I began to feel that perhaps others could feel me and understand. Secondly, perhaps someone could even relate to my struggles, and maybe I could reach someone. Maybe I could show one person that they are not in it alone. Lastly, even though I am not a psychologist or a mental health specialist, maybe in my own little way I could help raise awareness on a topic that too often is swept under our rugs.

I now would like to address another form of struggle, one that so many of us face, and that is the struggle of finding our purpose. Not only our purpose, but who we are, and the pursuit of becoming who we are meant to be. Pursuing a dream or an ambition is one thing entirely unto itself, but pursuing who we truly are is the true quest of life. For the true union that we all seek is not one that is found in a relationship, a career, success, or wealth, but it is the union with *ourselves* that we truly seek. For true victory is victory over oneself. This book is for the lost. This book is for the individual who is struggling in their search for their true identity, their happiness, and ultimate destiny. I say to you, keep seeking, and you shall find....*yourself.*

1st Offense is my *ode to the struggling*, and yes, it is also my love letter to the *Dreamers*. Where would this world be without it's dreamers? I'll answer that with this; without the dreamers this world would still be flat, no man would have ever walked on the surface of the moon, and no one would be able to travel by flight. We would be without technological advancements, and void of artistic expression. We would be, simply *void*, forever in the stone age. Dreamers I say to you, that whatever your dream takes the shape of, continue to believe in what God put in your heart. Continue to strive for it by placing one foot in front of the other. Day by day, patience for patience, adding strength to strength, keep persevering. Yes it will be difficult, but know this, everyday we stand on the shoulders of giants who persevered and scaled the highest heights to accomplish wonders. Men and women who created *realities* from *dreams*, and the world is better for it. So keep dreaming, stay inspired and keep your faith.

Lastly, this book is titled *1st Offense: The Beginning of the End*. Reader, you may be asking yourself, *what offense?* Well, five years ago I got myself into some trouble with the law for hustling marijuana, I was arrested, served a year of probation and it was my 1st (*and only*) offense. Hence, *1st Offense*. In a literal sense, this book is a first offense for the fact that it is my first publication. On a deeper level, it is my attempt to turn a negative offense into a positive one. Which brings me to your next question, *The Beginning of the End* of what, and *why so serious?* In life, each of us has a specific internal struggle that is tailor made to fit us inch for inch, seam for seam. Each of us has a riddle to unravel, a puzzle to solve, and a labyrinth to navigate. My tailor made struggle has consisted of the following; self-defeat, failure, procrastination, fear, even self-betrayal, low self-esteem and self-unworthiness, self-doubt, loneliness, etc. This book hales the *beginning of the end* of these things, and ushers in the *beginning* of a new belief in myself. The *end* of self-inflicted wounds, the *end* of involving myself in toxic situations and relationships, the *beginning* of positive change, self-actualization, and the *beginning of starting over*.

I have been waiting over a decade to say this, so without further ado, ladies and gentlemen I proudly present to you my first written work, *1st Offense: The Beginning of the End.*

-EMAJINAY

"Poetry is very subjective."
-JAMES EARL JONES

PART 1
1st OFFENSE
YOUTH & TIME

eGinnings

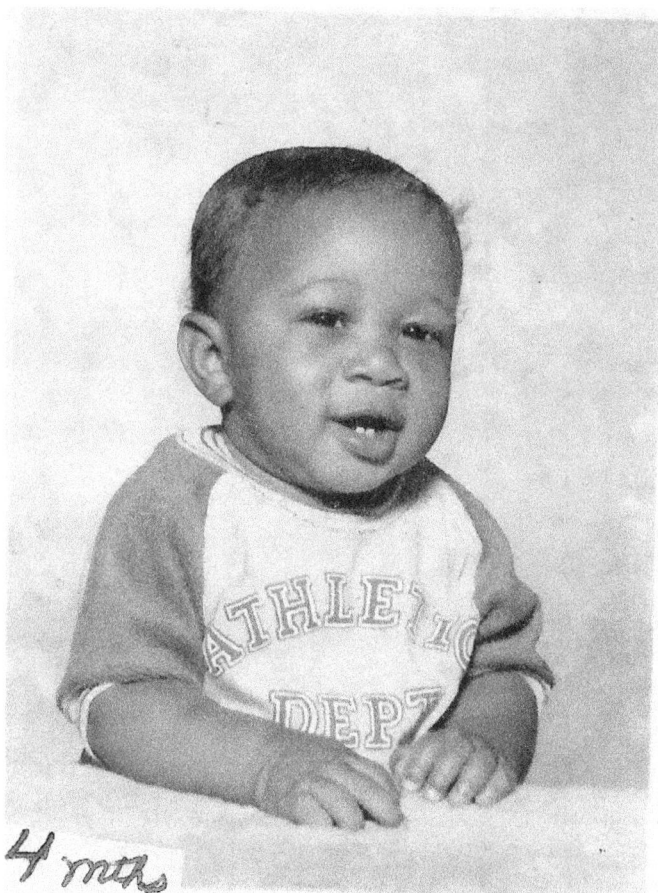

4 mths

EMAJINAYSHAUN

I'm just a sperm who grew legs,
Two arms, a midsection n' a head,
With a brain that developed.
That engulfs all the creativity that a mind can envelope,
Then I use one of my two hands
to spell it and a mouth to tell it.

Been tryin' to achieve, but I've been repellin' repellants,
Negatin' negativity that settled like a sediment,
Overcoming is like tryin' to win a settlement!
I'm the truth but lies in my mind got me forgettin' it,
Doubtin' n' second guessin' it,
Searchin' for my destiny when I'm standin' next to it!

Blessed from the onset,
Beyond blessed and beyond set,
Fly as a bomb jet, as bomb as bomb gets,
Stood on deck but I hadn't turned it on yet,
Underachieved like I wasn't allowed yet,
Lost sight of my object, started to get out less
n' I needed n' outlet,
To outlet stress that I wore out like an outfit,
Been writing for yrs n' it ain't all out yet,
I'm like a project, I'm a work in progress,
I got a lot to let out my chest, no doubt; I guess.
Sometimes I stress, in distress n' in duress, ponder n' guess,
Where a meal n' a dolla's gonna come from next,
All of these problems, all of these tests
in a trek n' quest for ultimate success drawin' n' writtin' text!

I create fire but I choke on the smoke!

I'm flat broke like a hobo with no hope who can't cope,
Strung out on coke n' dope in a cardboard box
Bound by duck tape n' ropes,
Socks soggy n' soaked with holes in his soul n' coat.
All for what and why?
See, the world was once void n' broke.
It took God 7 days to create somethin' beautiful,
Somethin' unmovable, viewable, majestically unusual,
Effiecient n' usable, melodic n' musical,
Somethin' suitable for art to dwell in.
This art dwells in my skin.
This art dwells within.

The ultimate artist created me to deliver art to others,
For children, fathers, n' mothers, sisters n' brothers,
Art to uncover n' discover with one another!
Emajinay wanna be diversified, art personified,
One day I'll arise,
N' my life will coincide with the one I see in my mind's eye.
Cause in it I have a vision,
N' when I come home to my crib
N' revisit all that I did,
I witness my dreams n' fruition,
From when since I was a kid n' was actin' out for attention,
Always knew I had a mission,
N' I spent everyday wishin' if
I could use it with good intention,
I'd provide a better livin'
For my Mama cookin' in the kitchen.
N' in my vision I see it all,
From the big to the small,
N' if I pursue it I can get it all.
I thank the Lord for blessin' me with a gift so tall,

I didn't get it from a mall or a auction hall,
Or 1-800 call,
I got it from the creator of the stars and universal laws,
N' when I think about it I have to pause,
Drop my jaws n' give praise n applause,
That in God's eyes somethin' special he saw,
That when He wrote my life contract;
He threw in a talent clause.
The rock's on my court, I just gotta have the balls,
To withdraw my head from the fog that chokes
my dreams like smog.
The sky is the limit,
Can't nothin' diminish it,
Possibilities infinite, n' now I'm all about gettin' it,
I'ma see my vision all the way through till I finish it,
Gotta take what's rightfully mine n' never relinquish it.

I ain't in a race, ain't in a hurry see,
but I'm urgent see, movin' with a urgency!
Urgent, Urgent, EMERGENCY!!
Urgent that I keep surging, dissectin' my life like a surgeon,
It's "impertant" I stay pertinent, strivin' for perfect,
I ain't caught up in the circus, I ain't watchin' hoes twerkin',
I got my head down workin' behind a closed curtain,
cause it's one thing that I know is certain,
Time waits for no man so I ain't gonna wait,
I got an appointment with destiny n' fate n' I can't be late.
I keep my dates, I keep pace, I can write at my own pace,
N' my pace'll set the pace for any other pace,
Tryin' to race n' the same space n' place,
I don't flow fast cause I want people to understand me,
Don't care about how flashy it sounds or how flashy it looks,
I want a kid to pick up a book like;

Hey brotha' look!
This Emajinay got sumthin' real to say,
N' I dig em' cause he say it in real kinda' way!
I want kids to say Emajinayshaun liberated minds,
Cause real talk; Imagination liberated *MINE!!!*
Einstein said imagination is
even more important than knowledge,
So if you get your Masters and you walk outta college,
If you can't imagine where you wanna be,
Then your ass'll be jobless!

My imagination gave me my gift
and the ability to do what I do,
My imagination gave me so much
that it gave me my name too.
In Greek poem means to make or create.
I'm a poet.
A maker & a creator.
Made in the image of The Creator.
My name is Emajinayshaun.

ABOUT ME

I hardly party like hardy har har hardly,
I'm hardly or never at a bar,
N' it's partly cause' I did it all!
N' that ain't where my heart be!
I'm home with my precious darling,
who I'd die for in a heartbeat!
I'm workin' hard I'm workin' hard weeks!
But I clown like I'm Chris Farley!
Pardon me if any a' this is dis-jarring!
Write me off n' you can discard me!
But I avoid the type of garbage
from my past that usually scarred me!
I just try to live a little more smart see,
spend my time bein' artsy,
N' I bet any amount of money
you didn't know those parts about me!

People think I lack direction n' motivation n' that sort'a junk!
But do you know I looked into being a sperm donor once?!
But cause I wasn't a doctor or a shrink the clerk
said I wasn't up to snuff!
I just wanted to play my part and stimulate the population,
Nay Sayers can Nay-Say and say what they may,
but I say that's *motivation!!*
Lookin' at me sideways for my lack of a college education!
Never mind that I'm a dude good with pictures n' words,
Formulatin' verbs into some of
the realist truth you ever heard!
Say that I've been an underachiever for most of my life,
you may be right!
Even go as far to say I've taken life

for granted n' taken it light!
Alright.
Yeah, I've never added up, never had enough,
never been standout'ish, never stood out in a crowd,
Self-esteem is low, it's hard to believe in myself,
I have very few friends, I just be by myself,
I sleep by myself, watch TV by myself,
hard to be jolly when your life is melancholy,
and that melancholy mood takes over my body.
Bittersweet an then it's sour,
Never been the man of the minute, let alone the hour,
How does it feel to be known but unknown?
Alone.
I alone get by alone, I live my life alone,
Everything I do is on my own,
and I alone will inevitably die alone.
Cumbersome I have become,
I have become so cumbersome,
I see cars as they come an I wanna crawl up under one.

I'm lonely and strange.
No one remembers my name cause I'm strange.
People don't treat me the same cause I'm strange.
The uttered words you've heard, don't misconstrue,
see I'm slightly disturbed, not aloof but slightly perturbed.

BUT THERE'S SO MUCH MORE TO KNOW
THEN WHAT YOU SEE WHEN YOU ON FACEBOOK!
LOOK INTO MY EYES, READ MY FACE N' TAKE A LOOK!
NEVER JUDGE A COVER,
TURN THE PAGE N' READ THE BOOK!

PEOPLE'LL THINK THEY KNOW THE STORY

WHEN THEY CATCH ME, WHEN THEY SPOT ME!
CONFUSE ME WIT A LOTTA' STUFF,
A LOTTA' JUNK THAT'S NOT ME!
DON'T DEFEND ME OR COMMEND ME,
NO PRETENDING WHEN BEFRIENDING,
SIMPLY TAKE THE TIME TO KNOW THE MAN,
GET TO KNOW ME FOR WHO N' WHAT I AM!

I'm being honest with you, I'm being honest with myself,
If for nothing more or nothin' less than better health,
Thru honesty I'll perhaps be healed,
Like an open vault I'm unconcealed,
My thoughts and feelings now revealed,
At times my actions may not show it,
But you're listening to the loneliest poet,
My time is up, my secret's out, and now everybody knows it.

As I Walk

As I'm walking my mind is talking,
bout' my life and how things tend to mess up so often.
As I'm walking my mind is talking,
contemplating suicide as I approach this bridge,
seriously thinking bout' jumpin' off in-to,
this river I won't land soft in.
Like a tiger crouching, like a dragon hidden,
can I fly into the wind then float my way to heaven?
While I'm walking my mind is talking,
dissecting and asking questions;
When I die will I get a new life?
Will there be a resurrection?

Feet moving, chest heaving, my mind is speaking,

mind's eye open searching for answers I'm still seeking,
the sky's out of reach, but I keep reaching.
As I walk by myself, I talk to myself,
I'm mad at myself,
I can't seem to live with myself.
The line I'm walking is thin,
I'm talking within and a war rages therein,
and God as my witness I want my better side to win,
But I'm livin' in sin,
a whirlwind I'm in,
and I just want it to end.
While I'm walking, my mind is talking.

MENTALLY MUTE @ *20 yrs old*

Noise. Full of noise. The world is full of noise.
But yet it seems like all I hear is my own voice.
Brought into this noisy world
and didn't have a choice.
Heart is racing, palms moist, I'm a nervous wreck.
The burdens of my life weigh heavily upon my chest,
time to find myself before I have no time left,
constantly worried, I worry I might worry myself to death,
I'm dying for change but I'm impatient,
only 20 years old but I feel so freakin' ancient.
There is war waging within' n' again,
God as my witness I want my better side to win,
Good and Evil in eternal dispute,
what makes it worse is that
I've become mentally mute.

Light. Full of light. The world is full of light.

But yet it seems like all I tend
to see are dim corridors of darkness,
Life's been sucked outta me,
and there's no energy I can harness,
Praying for the Lord to shine divine light upon my eyes,
increase my focus to an ultimate high,
turn up the sharpness,
cause it's hard to find my way
when I'm traveling in darkness.
Mentally mute, tackled,
I'm mentally shackled by my fears,
isolated for years from family and peers,
no longer can I escape the real with a blunt or a beer,
Eyes open, vision clear, looking up the road of my life
and the end is nowhere near,
It's all ahead of me, destiny,
so make the best of life while I'm here,
Stay strong and shed no tears,
Grab the bull by the horns and life by the balls,
Sky's the limit, surpass it,
And never put all my eggs in one basket.

Love. Full of love. Oh this world is full of love.
Lord, send love down from up above; full of love.
But I have little for myself,
I know that smokin' that crap ain't good for my health,
But I'm stressed out, sometimes I
feel like killing myself,
I'm deep in the depths,
a far cry from glory and wealth.
U see the world is full of love,
and the world is full of life,
But I ain't livin' mine right,

Night turns to day then back into night,
But love comes with the light,
So everything'll be alright,
Cause the world is full of love
and the world is full of light,
But until then, until when?
This war wages within n' again
God as my witness I want my better side to win.
Good and Evil in eternal dispute,
Lord awaken me, I'm mentally mute.

MURKYWATERS

Murky waters, oceans and streams,
Hard to envision my dreams,
the darkside clouds everything,
I feel polluted like R. Kelly's wet dreams,
Diluted like Mike Tyson's career in the ring,
I'm claustrophobic, I can't breathe,
Frustrations emit from my pores like hot steam,
Gotta keep a cool head,
Gotta keep it together,
Keep myself from blowing up,
Gotta release all this pressure,
Be free from this choke-hold,
No mo' holds; I'm barred,
Life's gotten a little more relaxed but it's still freakin' hard,
But I'm focused on the moment,
and getting back on course,
Focused on restoring total balance to the force,
But see my ship ain't sturdy,
at times it's herky jerky,

Situation isn't perty,
But I won't let nothing scur me,
I just keep forging ahead in these waters,
So dirty and murky.

I was guilty by association,
Associatin' wit peculiar faces in peculiar places,
Many times I found myself facin' peculiar situations,
Made questionable decisions
that raised a lot of questions,
And caused a lot of 2nd guessin',
The Lord's steadily testing,
To teach me life long lessons,
I'm tryin' to live in the present,
Cause I wanna receive His blessings,
But right now my life's outta
shape like Tommy LaSorda,
It's sorta-sorta,
Discombobulated, disheveled and outta order,
Walkin' a tight line, tip toeing on the border,
Tryin' not to fall over,
Fightin' to keep myself from
plungin' beneath the murky waters.
These waters I'm drowning in,
And it's more like quicksand,
making it harder for me to swim,
A gravitational pull drags me deeper within',
It started at my waist and now it's up to my chin,
Sinkin' by the second, my outcome is lookin' grim,
Won't make it I reckon, chances of survival lookin' thin,
Have I givin' it my all? Or all that I have I gave?
Is this how it all ends?
Layin' face down in a watery grave?

MESSAGE IN A BOTTLE

Now's the time, window of opportunity; Open.
The words that I've written now need 2 be felt n' spoken,
I'm sick of feelin' broken in this cloudy room smokin'
Choakin on this blunt that I'm tokin',
Life's gone from nitty 2 gritty,
I'm tired of feeling broken,
In this pity I soak in,
Feelin' like croakin,
It's hard for these words to be told in rhymes,
I get these feelings at times, these feelings inside,
I can't explain or define,
The complexity of this Rubik's Cube in my mind,
But if it's alright with you I'll give it a try,
Just clear the mind, open the mind,
Sit back, relax and watch my words fly.

Gotta change today in order to change tomorrow,
Gotta find happiness to replace the sorrows,
Gotta fill the void space that feels so hollow,
This is my Message in A Bottle.

Been through a lot for the worse or better,
Been tarred been feathered,
I've experienced many climates, I've been weathered.
Went through this and that
Now I'm ready for whatever,
Lord don't let me crumble,
Help me keep it all together,
Cause nobody lives forever
It's now or never.

Birthday just passed on the 28th,
You'd think all is well and great but it ain't,
My priorities are whack and I can't get em' straight,
It's like the devil's coaxin' me n' I keep fallin' for the bait,
Feelin' like I've been beat,
Causin' me to retreat into moments of solitude,
That deepen my melancholy mood,
I'm growing more confused I don't know what to do,
Which road will I choose?
Which path will I follow?
Fear and confusion are hard pills to swallow,
That's why I've placed my plea in this bottle,
Plugged it with my cork and tossed it in the ocean,
Tides washing up on my feet
As I watch it floatin'.

Walk away from the shore n' sunshine pourin' on my skin,
Hope filling up within',
From rock bottom now I gotta climb to the tip of it,
God blessed me with life and I gotta keep livin' it,
Love's been givin' to me so I gotta keep givin' it,
Gotta live life to the fullest;
To the end of it.

16 BARS

This flow was flowing through my
mind like a runnin' faucet,
It was too good to toss it so
I wrote it down before I lost it.
Driving home n' my mind was in a slight haze,
Then I reminisced on my HS days,

My HS ways chillin' with my homies in our little city,
Chilly outside, temp dippin' below 50,
Chilly-willy but we kept warm with
some sips of Henny, actin' silly,
Broke as a joke without a penny in me,
Pullin' our pockets out like rabbit ears
to see who's the brokest,
Pocket lint fallin' out our pockets like roaches,
Got a quick laugh n' quickly shifted our focus,
Like let's see how loud n' rowdy we can get
until the cops approach us!
16 bars for cats n' 16 cars,
Drive by 16 bars!
Sippin' liquor n' beer outta 16 jars!
Ride around for 16 hrs
Lookin' like 16 stars!
Broke as hell, all we got
Between us is 16 dollars,
But even though it was all we had,
That 16 was all ours!
N' to all of us
16 seemed like stardom!
On top of the world
N' Worthy of 16 pardons!
I remember 16 seemed like an eternity,
N' positive that when it came
my life would come 2gthr perfectly!
But changes were disturbin' me!
The pitcher threw some curves @ me!
Self-conscious certainly hurtin' me,
Workin' me overtime!
Like demons were lurkin' in me!
Tossin' n' jerkin' me!

Rug burnin' n' "turfin'" me!
Workin' me purposely, assertively!
Hurlin' me n' swirlin' me
Down a drain leadin' to doubt;
My self-esteem was desertin' me,
It turned on me!
N' I forgot that I had worth in me!
The worth that God had birthed in me!
Damn; I was like a pin cushion,
Felt like all I had was dirt in me!
Young wild but not free, I recall the wild in me,
Wild as a child could possibly be,
Spur of the moment mixed with monotony,
Without a plan for the future I was scared of the future,
Felt like I had nothin' to get me movin',
Just pursuin' the will-o'-the wisps of "youthful limitless"
Youthful limits eclipsed, I was losin' my innocence,
Youth is wasted on the young,
quote never used ta' make any sense,
But when I reminisce I see I put nothin' useful into it!!
Can it be that it was all so simple then,
all so simple when,
Did the same things so them
things could get "did" again.

I remember when 16 seemed far,
N' I when I got there 16 seemed hard!
At 16 my esteem seemed scarred!
At 16 I dreamed n' schemed hard!
N' although all of my dreams seemed large,
Reinforcements seemed sorta' sparce,
N' all my dreams seemed far!
Like my dreams were on Mars!

16 had me jarred!
16, n' barred like I was behind 16 bars!

It was hard to see past 16,18, 21,
It was 21 n' done for some, R.I.P to the ones,
For me 21 was when it all begun,
I recall being young was less than fun,
I recollect on all I've done,
Bad mistakes yeah I've made some,
More than one n' more than some,
I've been foolish n' I've been dumb,
I swear I've put the Tweedle-Dee
Inside the Tweedle-Dum!!
But nevertheless I was 16 n' glistening with dreams,
which seemed hard to grapple,
this thing tackle slippin', it seemed hard to tackle,
Drifting caught out in midstream,
Up a creek without a paddle,
What to do with this gleam, this dream, I was baffled,
Dreams flickering on a silkscreen ready to dazzle,
16, pristine as the Sistine Chapel,
16 a sweet theme, light the 16 Candles.

FADE TO GREY
(BLACK BOY VITILIGO)

Papa was a lonely stone who gathered a lot of moss,
A strict dude with strict rules to follow
But he was the boss!
I didn't live up to the expectations
He was settin' n' I wasn't behaving
Up to par like he expected,
Pops had me feelin' neglected
When all I wanted was his acceptance
But I could never get it,
So I kept it movin like forget it!
If its attention n' acceptance
That I want then I'ma get it!
Anything I wanted to do I went n' did it!
Didn't hide it I never hid it,
Couldn't even if I tried so I didn't,
A school kid with big balls,
Ran ramped in the halls,
Put outta study hall,
From the office to detention hall,
N' I did it all just to get attention from ya'll!
Did it work, naw, not at all.
I landed in a program for the Severely Behavioral
Handicapped teenagers.
SBH.
Ridin' the short bus wasn't that great!
I was never voted most likely to
Rise to a position of high class livin',
But rather most likely to falter n' fail n' fade into oblivion,
I was never voted most likely to succeed,
But probably most likely to be the 1st human

To overdose on some weed!

In 99' Mama n' me moved to a new part of town,
Left my ol' man for a while n' outta our ol' place,
Left my ol' friends n' started feeling outta place,
I had never been amongst so many of my own before.
Like hey, I'm in the hood,
Toto we ain't in Kansas no more,
From Lake Elementary to Shore, Memorial,
Mentor HS, to Harvey doors,
When them kids saw me I swear
them jaws dropped n' hit the floor.
Pierced up, geared up, my gear preppy n' near tough!
Kid smoother than suede,
I had highlights in my waves!
It threw niggas' off but it was just the
style of the click in the burbs
Where I used to stay back in the day.
But a lotta cats started backin' away.
Like, is he black or white?
Michael Jackson told us that
That doesn't matter right?
B, you act a little dark,
N' you act a little light,
You the whitest black dude I've ever known in all my life!
So technically that would make my color grey, right!
I heard it from black n' white kids a like!
I wouldn't lie to you I promise,
I'm Lee Thomas!
I have Vitiligo!! Right bro?
Check how the complex complexity
of my complexion might grow!
I might go into a whole other sector n'

section on the color spectrum!
See me in another light though!
I'ma end up poka-dotted;
I'm spotted!
N' when they spot me they like here he come!
N' they say to one another;
"When you see spot RUN!"
They spot me by the way I'm actin'
or by hearin' my vernacular,
N' they see me as different but never nothin' spectacular!
Treat me like I'm Dracula!
Reachin' for they garlic n' they cloves n' they dagger or,
Crucifix for crucifixion just to add to my affliction,
Cause I don't fit the fixed description,
of the jurisdiction's fixed depiction!
I may be wrong, I may be fishin',
But that's just my mixed opinion!
Listen...I'm the invisible man.
I'm stand off-ish,
I stand off n' often I stand often alone,
Often at home, like Macaulay Culkin.
I'm home.
Life's in a fast lane that surrounds me,
Lapin' around me,
In a time lapse clamped by a tight clasp in a glass trapped,
Watchin' time pass, time collapsin' around me!
The confines of my past grabs n' bounds me,
Like I'm in an Anaconda's grasp wrappin' around me!
Emajinay; enigma
Entangled, entrapped,
Encaged in cage, enveloped,
Been fed up,
Sometimes feel like I been set up,

By set backs disguised as blessings
That set me back to the set ups,
That kept my head up,
N' forced me to never let up,
Get knocked down I gotta get up
N' I never forget it nah
The person I was before,
Who I am now n' the person I'm lookin' for!
Entrapped, enveloped, inverted, inserted into introverted.
You get too close, won't get a close up man,
Cause I close up man,
Protect myself before it blows up man,
Leave a hole in my chest like a donut man,
I'm a faceless man on Earth,
Feel like life chased n' erased me off the face of the Earth!
Walked me to the edge where I fell off.
N' any promise that I had, or any self-worth,
Fate erased it at birth,
Don't mean to sound faithless n' burnt,
But it's all I can relay or say n' it hurts.
Tis' I ya'll, the spotted one.
The jaded, the faded, the tainted, the pigment challenged,
Improperly painted spotted Dalmatian.
The sum of a black n' white past, that I recall on a lonely day,
Recall on moonlit nights in my crib like a stowaway,
It's all a part of me although I wish
that I could make it go away,
But it's imprinted n' branded to me like
A scar a surgeon couldn't take away,
So at night I draw my blanket over my spots after
I pray n' rest my head n' lay,
Take a deep breath into my chest,
Close my eyes n' fade to grey.

Dear _ _ _,

Dear blank space_
Blank space_
N' another blank space.
I can't fill the letters in that very blank space,
most nights when I dream I can still your face,
Except it's surreal n' the reality's replaced.

You see, in that world we're
Everything we should've been,
Everything we could've been,
n' it's all surreal but then again,
It's as real as it gets,
n' as real as it's ever been.

We take road trips.
Travel to far away places.
See different things
n' see far different faces.

We laugh together.
Tell stories n' cling to each moment
as if it's our last.
In my dreams you smile, n' I long to see you.
I follow you in & out of every room in the house.
n' we play hide n go seek, and cat n' mouse.

In my dreams I grow up before your very eyes.
We skip rocks on the beach.

You tell me I'm your favorite straight "A" student.
As I glide like a kid on a pair of Heely's to accept my diploma,

I see you in the sea of faces of my HS auditorium,
Tears swelling up in your eyes,
Your heart swelling with pride,
N' I can read your lips as you lean to the people
at your side n' with a gleam in your eyes you whisper;
That's my boy.
N' when we meet outside
You hug as me as if I'm the Prodigal Son
N' you tell me that you're so very proud of me.
You reach in your jacket pocket
n' pull out a pair of shiny new keys,
I ask, "Who's are those?"
And you say that they're for me.
"You deserve it. Knock em' dead!"
you tell me with a proud grin.
I yell out 20 thank you's & 20 I love you's
as I turn to hop n' my new gift, when you say;
"Hold on. I don't mean knock em' dead literally now!
N' take it easy wit' dem girls,
I ain't ready for NO grandbabies!"
"Aww, not even one!" I joke with a sheepish smile.
"My boy." you say.
Then your face fades away,
n' I roll off my pillow n' awake to a new day.
I awake to the real thing.
I awake to my real dream.
Our relationships like two brackets
with nothin' in between.
Outside of these dreams
we don't have anything.
Except questions.
How can a boy grow to be a man,
How can a boy learn to make the

tough decisions that only a man can make,
N' only a man can teach?
That only 3 blank spaces can teach?
What was your vision for me?
What kind of a man did you hope I would become?
We never shared much together,
Who are you? Really.
Shit, who am I?
Am I all that you thought I'd be?
Are you proud of me?
Do you ever think, of me?
Your boy.
Your son.

Three blank spaces.
Three very blank spaces.
My heart. My mind. My world.
It breaks my heart when I reminisce,
Ain't you an engineer n' a mechanic,
Ain't you s'posed to fix shit?

Dear blank space_
Blank space__
n' another blank space.
All you placed in my life was a bunch of blank space.
With brackets at each end n' with nothing in between,
And the only time I fill the space,
is when I see you in my dreams.

WORRIER'S ANONYMOUS @ *22 yrs old*

Help me I'm trapped inside my beautiful mind,
I can't get out cause the exit is so hard to find,
I long to be comfortable in my own skin,
Cause immense potential and promise is wrapped up within',
So much to bring to the table and so much to give,
My patience is wearin' thin with this life that I live,
My progress is hendered by the stress my mind renders,
Can I get back on my feet and start over like a beginner?
Press on and step on, no let up, no surrender?
Lord knows, cause I arise with the
sunrise with worries on my mind,
I worry morning, noon, and night,
constantly worried all the time,
My mind is like a chat room for Worrier's Anonymous,
Always receiving visitors, no matter what time it is,
I worry over anything and stuff that don't exist,
It don't matter the situation or what the drama is,
Sometimes I worry for no reason,
I don't know what my problem is.
Once in awhile my worries'll go away,
And I'll start feeling relaxed and start feeling ok,
Then outta nowhere it'll tap me on my shoulder like, "HEY!"
"Remember all that crap you was
worried about the other day?"
I stress a lot over my woman,
like maybe she don't wanna see me,
Or maybe she doesn't need me,
Or perhaps she might be cheating, or planning on leaving,
I worry I might worry myself into submission,
till there's nothin' left of me,
Man, if I don't stop this it's gonna be the death of me.

Say I do but I don't,
Say I will but I won't,
Say I wouldn't but I would,
Say I shouldn't when I should,
I couldn't when I could,
Sick n' tired of singin' shoulda-coulda-woulda's,
Talkin' bout stuff I woulda and shoulda done when I coulda.
Rememberin' a time when I shoulda been dead,
Coulda been six feet under but I'm breathin' instead,
In the land of the living till it's my time to go,
22 years young and I'm blessed to even be this old,
So I cherish each breath cause life is precious like gold,
Many come and go, and many a life has ended abruptly,
Premature and suddenly, that's why I live humbly,
Try to live a righteous life before death comes for me,
Cause death serves no warrant and comes without notice,
So I gotta use my time wisely and try to stay focused.
No tellin' how my life will end,
No tellin' when.
Wanna live to see my daughter turn
18 but I may not even live till then,
So nothin' for nothin' and for all it's worth,
I've been blessed with life from the date of my birth,
I gotta cherish every second here on God's green Earth,
And remember that life's a gift and not a curse.
And yeah,
P.S- Stop worrying so damn much.

LOOKING

BOTH WAYS

SUM OF A FALL

I being of unsound mind
And weary body barely
remember where I've been,
N' I don't know where I'm goin',
On a long road to Nowhere
N' I haven't been to Somewhere yet.
Split personality attacked by an attached Incubus
That's linked to us!
N' one day I woke up n' died,
Couldn't feel nothin',
Dead but still alive.
My body told me I was
but my heart n' mind said otherwise.
At times I've felt like my life's
been a half truth n' 3 quarters of a lie.
A bad concept of self
became my new truth in disguise.

A lot a' times wisdom's
derived from being unwise.
Well in that case I should
be the wisest man alive, no jive!
I've lost sight of my truth,
Values n' aptitudes,
I'm a happless dude,
In a happless mood,
Sad n' bruised n' a bad attitude.
When I can afford n' stand ta' care,
In my mirror standing bare,
But I can't stand the glare of
standin' there face 2 face with

and aware as I stand n' stare at the
unbearable likeness standin' there;
Two of us n' I can't stand the pair!
Being brutally honest with myself;
It's hard n' rare n' I must admit
I FEEL pretty damn bare.
N' I'm still unsure as to
Whether or not
I look good with it all off.

A fall from grace ain't a fall that's soft!
It's a fall that hurts n' a fall that costs!
A fall that hurts the whole way down,
No parachutes or windgliders
to slow it down!
Ain't no way around
the fact that I'm earthward bound,
at such a startling speed that my certain death
Now becomes a sound!
I could hear it in a sense,
n' clouds didn't slow my descent,
and the ground is unforgiving.
A rough way to come back to life
n' back to reality,
somehow I survived n' escaped from casualty.
Now I'm hopin' to find
solace and redemption at rock bottom.
I'm back on my feet, clear headed
with some problems ta' solve,
finding a new trajectory
n' a new way to revolve,
Live up to my Calling,
N' accept the cause of the call

To evolve.
All of this is the best way
To sum it up n' add it all,
I guess all I'm sayin' ta' y'all is; I am the sum of a fall.

HALOGEN HAZE

Up late with my lady,
Gazing at the afterlives of stars,
Pondering on how far they truly are.
If what they say is true,
With scientific proof; no guessin',
If light can truly reach through in less than a second,
Can my wish transport itself back to that light source
in the same length of time?!

See right now I'm at a point where I don't know if
Things are comin' together or just fallin' apart.
My life's in limbo, but I've spent most
of my life that way anyway,
So it should feel good to me by now.
Pedaling against the grain.
Against life's vicissitudes and constant changes,
I've pedaled so long I'm worn out n' deflating like a slow leak!
Hard to speak, hard to holler,
when I'm drownin' with a mouth full a' water!
In my ocean of demise,
drifting away with the currents of my mind.

I've been pulled under before, I feel like the weight
of the world on my shoulders.
N' that's a weight I cannot grip, my life is on an acid trip!

Seein' tracers in a halogen haze, befuddled n' dazed,
A hell of a faze of life to be in!
I'm out here with nothin' 2 lose and a world to gain.
I'm ready for somethin' organic to take root
n' govern my life n' get me rolling!
So in the words of a novelist;
Rock bottom now becomes the
foundation on which I must rebuild my life.
This is my future.
My present and past.
This is it, every component, every exponent,
every variable in chronological sequence.
From the start and on through to now;
Every failure,
Every moment of elation n' celebration,
Every detention n' suspension,
Every day that I played hooky,
Every time I got laid,
Every girl who rejected me,
Every job I had n' lost,
Every clam bake,
Every good or bad date,
Every bowel movement,
Cough n' cold,
Depression n' agorophobia,
Every moment of indecision,
Every **choice.**
Adds up to the life I'm livin';
Now.

It's on now.
Time to blow up or blow it!
I have to find gears that I'm not even sure I have,

but believe are in me.
This is a prophecy a lifetime in the making,
N' now it's time to fulfill it n' it's mine for the taking!
Time to break down walls that need breaking!
Walls that obstructed the view of my mind's eye,
N' had misleading hieroglyphics n' graffiti inscribed,
Lines of BS that had me bribed!
It all was a lie, why cry, why ask why?
I tried ta' try but it all went awry,
But I ain't gonna watch my life fly by, I'll survive!

I'm ordained for more than ordinary,
Life's full of the mundane,
But also loaded with extraordinary,
My life has been a little void n' I need more to carry,
I'm trapped in a spritual mortuary,
Modern day Lazurus; Laid to a board n' buried.
Now I rise, to strive n' stride,
Swallow my little pride,
Toss the empty wallet aside.
They say procrastination is the fear of success,
Time to be an adult ta' atone for my mistakes; mea culpa.
Ain't got a' lot a' pride to swallow;
It's a small gulp a' meaningless taste!
God forgive me for my previous ways,
Please believe me I'm fazed,
Please provide some clarity n' relief from this Haze!

PRESENCE

This moment...
I can see it.

Here.
Now.
In this; moment.
This present.
This, future.

I can hear the voice of Eckhart Tolle,
Lecturing a PBS audience on the
Importance of presence.
Now is all we have.
It is all there is, or ever was,
Have no concern for the past or future;
There is only NOW.
For the past is not but a story,
The Future does not exist.
It is not here, we are not there.
And when we do actually
Arrive in this, so called future,
It is now NOW!!
The future is NOW!!
We are already in it!
There is only Now.
I ask you to focus on Now.
To be in THIS moment.
And so many of you, you say to yourselves;
What?
What moment?
There are SO many moments!

But what you must realize and understand
Is that there is NO moment but NOW.
There is only;
THIS moment.

So now.
Right now.
Right here.
In this present.
In this future.
This now.
This, moment… I can see it all.
All of my past and future
Flashing before my mind's eye in this Moment.
Right now.
"I'm screwed!"

I can feel the cold steel of a barrel,
Firmly pressed flush against my temple,
Synapses and electric impulses,
fire off, simultaneously linked
to my thoughts in the moment.
My mind processing data at the speed of light
Right down to the most minut detail.
My cash n' the stash; take it!
But before you take ME away,
Just allow ME to say,

Like s'il vous plait,
Grant a lil' lee-a-way,
I made a hell of a mistake,
But I need to be free today!
Take my paraphernalia even take my TV away!

I ain't got no E&J but you can even take my DNA!
Read me my mirandas,
But just allow me to pray!
Read the mirandas;
Go 'head n' read em'!
But lemme keep my freedom!
Don't take my freedom!
Don't take my freedom!
They say time is money,
But days are priceless n' I really need em'!

I can hear the squad cars rushin' in to hasten my demise.
Dope stuffed in my pockets to their pleasure n' surprise,
"The Boys" drag me before "Your Honor"
to be facin' some time!
Locked up to lose precious **moments** of my life!

I can hear it all right **now**.
The "one" phone call to a so n' so.
The conversations between bunks.
Goin' bunk to bunk talkin' junk,
Sharing stories about our "conjugal" visits!

Right now, I can see the consequences
of my actions in **THAT** future!
As I simultaneously reflect on the shoulda-coulda-woulda's
that I SHOULDA' done in **THAT** past!

They say thank God for **small** favors,
The way I see it, I thank God for **ALL** favors!

The past is just a ship that sailed!
The past is just a story,

And the S.S Story can never
be restored to her former glory.
And future conclusions are only illusions
So don't mix the two up n' don't confuse em'!
Every minute n' moment I have, I have to use em'!
Cause all I have is **NOW**!
All I've ever had is **NOW**!
This **now**.
Right **now**.
Right here.
In this past.
In this future.
In this **PRESENT**.
The Present is a *Present*,
and the presence is present.

THIRTY MILE MISTAKE

"THERE ONCE WAS A MAN WHO WALKED A CROOKED MILE."

How come I end up where I started?
How come I always end up where I'm from?
Bad decisions I've made,
That when it hit me n' after they were made,
I realized I made a 30 mile mistake.
Now that's when you travel ten miles in the wrong direction,
Then travel ten miles just to get back to where you started,
And finally another ten miles to get to where
your ass was supposed to be goin' in the 1st place!
Thirty miles.
I've traveled miles,
I've traveled miles in my mind,

Traveled miles till it seemed there were no miles left to find.
I take one step forward then take three steps back,
Then take one forward n' still don't know where I'm at!
Two steps toward a different position,
Then four steps back to where I was just sittin',
Sittin' wishin' I knew where I was goin' in the 1st place!
Land of the lost is the worst place,
From Ohio n' back to my birthplace,
Wishin' I'da gotten it right on the 1st take.
N' the further I travel down the wrong path
The harder it gets for me to find my way back,
Cause all the roads just start
lookin' the same as all the others,
N' I can't Google or Map Quest my way outta this one.
I'm just flat out lost!
N' everyone I try to get directions
from sends me in the wrong direction.
Why should I expect them to know where they are anyway?
They're right here in the same place as me!
Daddy always told me that birds of a feather flock together!
So there it is in a nutshell;
Me, nesting with a bunch of misguided pigeons,
Out here in flocks, migratin' to anywhere without cause
or any sense of direction.
We fall like feces from the skies,
on our long journey to nowhere.

Parties n' disjointed social gatherings;
Drinking it up, 40 oz. to my freedom,
Malt liquor n' blunts helped me find a way to escape,
N' get myself into a sublime state of mind,
Wakin' up only to find that I was
in the wrong places all the time!

Dope spots with thug types,
Movie theaters & in restaurants at night,
Sitting across from a lady I
couldn't be less interested in & vice versa!
Wakin' up in places I never heard of!
Workin' midnight shifts to avoid the light of day,
Seekin' out the best possible paths in
the worst possible ways.
I jumped at the beaconing call of anything.
The 1st proposition that sounded good to me,
I was off n' runnin', I'm often runnin',
off into somethin' that led often to nothin'!
Often with someone, I went any n' everywhere,
wherever I may roam,
but now I find myself on this journey all alone,
n' far from home, more than a hop, skip, n' a jump,
n' I could toss a million stones,
but I wouldn't even know the 1st direction to throw em' in!
I've gone wrong for far too long,
I gotta collect myself n' get my mind straight,
Retrace n' backtrack over my mistakes,
So I can be able to move forward n' escape!
My well's filled to the max,
Holdin' a fistful of tears n' welled up in the past.
I'm sending out an S.O.S,
Can't find my way outta this mess,
I'm all turned around,
and I don't know where I am, I can't really tell,
I must be somewhere under heaven,
n' I'm standin' over hell.
Guess I won't be finding where I'm looking for today!
Guess I gotta find MYSELF, before I find my WAY!

IT'S A SMALL WORLD

My world is small,
Infinitesimally small.
I can stand still in one place,
Turn 360 degrees and I'm back again.
Everywhere I go I keep bumpin' into MYSELF!!
I need to expand my world, it's imperative.
But 1st it's imperative that I *fix* my world.
This little frail world of mine.
For the fact that it no longer suits me.
Everyday I feel like a terd warmed over.
Tore up from the floor up,
My soul's cryin' out through my skin!
Pouring through my pours
Tryin' ta' tell me somethin' I suppose,
Maybe that in SO many different ways,
My life is wrong on SO many different levels.

It's like a snow-globe I'm in, n' I'm shook up,
Took up by the swirls n' twirls that spin.
Abandon all hope ye who enters here,
It's too cramped n' you wouldn't like it anyway.
My world's so small it's real easy to get around,
N' my world's so small, I can't believe it's really round.
I'm on flatlands looking for a better landscape
and better climate conditions.
Because my ozone's depleted, and
my atmosphere's heavily polluted with my own emissions.
This is my testament and my own admission.
I have neglected to be environmentally conscious
of the surroundings of my habitat
and the things that have habitation within me.

I need to discover and relocate to a
New world before the one I've created destroys me.
A place to start anew, a world of hope,
A world of promise, a world of change.
One much larger and more spacious,
One that offers room for new growth where I can flourish.
I must find this place.
I won't stop traveling until I arrive at my destination.
And perhaps, upon my arrival,
I'll discover that it's not such a small world after all.

VICIOUS CYCLE

Different people struggle with different afflictions,
Different predicaments, hardships, and addictions,
That become strongholds in our lives
and attach like extensions,
Some we share with others,
While others go unmentioned,
Some we tend to,
Others get no attention.
At times I feel like I'm weighed down
by a million paper weights,
Face down with my face plastered to a paper plate.
At times I feel like I'm sleepwalkin',
N' I gotta stop that crap;
'Cause sleep is like station breaks,
Dreams are like commercials,
I gotta wake up n' rejoin the program already in progress.
Yeah, you see cause I think I saw tomorrow; Yesterday.
I spend so much time stressin'
over what's ten miles down the road,

I tend to forget that my future is now,
My future is here.

But you see I'm caught in a vicious cycle,
N' trust me it ain't delightful,
N' I can't break loose,
No matter how hard I try to,
Fightin' bad habits,
A strenuous struggle I constantly fight through,
Time is against me,
Myself I can no longer lie to,
Time to stop singin' shoulda coulda woulda's,
All the things that I might do,
And get it all together,
Start livin' my life the way that I'd like to ,
Do what I'm assigned to do,
Get myself in alignment to the formation
that my stars align to,
Flow smooth with the flow of a Haiku,
Short but sweet, subtle but effective,
Achieving inner peace is my only objective,
But my behavior isn't reflective.
I'm caught in vicious cycle n' I hate it,
I'm caught in a vicious cycle n'
don't know how the hell I made it,
It's like firing away at a force field n I can't penetrate it,
It's a woeful feeling that I live day to day with,
My spirits tired, I'm sick n' tired;
this some crap I need to do away with.

My existence is obscured n' blurred like muffled words.
I keep livin' my days over like Taye Diggs,
Every time the Day Breaks,

Reconstructing everything I did in order to redirect my fate,
I live one day, then I live it again,
Then I relive that day all over again,
It's repetitious and hard to mend,
Knowing precisely how my day I'll spend,
How much longer will this cycle spin?
Will this day come to an end?
Will it ever?
N' if so, then when?
I am addicted to this cycle like cigarettes.
A pheen to the nicotine, change my name to Nick.
Hey, Nick a pheen!
I keep smokin' these cigarettes although I've
Said I've had enough n' when I say that I'ma quit,
I feel like I'm bluffin',
Sayin' this my last one right as I'm puffin',
Someone inject me with Nicoderm cause look; I'm strugglin'!
But see, a patch won't do, a patch won't help,
A patch can peel off land in hot water n' melt,
I need more than just patches,
I done torn so many different patches away,
From so many areas of my flesh,
I got sores from 10 yrs ago that still look fresh!
All these yrs tryin to patch up my shame,
My sadness, my fears, my anger n' worries,
Wrapping ace bandages around my abdomen
To halt any further amount of my self-esteem from escaping,
I've punctured my belly where my umbilical was,
N' pumped my soul full of Fix O' Flat!
Hopin' that when this tornado dies n' drops me off
From somewhere over the rainbow,
I'll still be full of some kind of hope,
Some kind of dream to hold tight to.

I've patched up my head n' corked my ears
To prevent bad spirits from gettin' in,
But in actuality I'm trappin' em' in
To the point that my heads 'bout to explode.
I'm patched up n' I need more,
Maybe some kinda serum,
Some kinda anecdote for my ills',
I'll take anything to cure em'!
Have em' surgically removed,
dowse em' with kerosene n' burn em'!
Take em' to a customer service department n' return em'!
Like this junk got me startin' to feel psychotic,
Here take this junk I'm no longer satisfied with this product!
It isn't fulfilling n' it's no longer fun,
Let me speak with the manager I demand a refund!
I'M DONE!!
I gotta drop the BS in the same way
I gotta drop them smokes,
'Cause up to this point life's been nothin' but a joke,
It's 7 degrees outside n' I'm freezin'
out here just for a few tokes,
For a few puffs,
Time to head back in cause my life ain't up to snuff,
Enough is enough!
I'm tired of this cycle,

So sick n' tired of my addiction to this cycle
Time to head back in n' close the door,
Stop lettin' the heat out cause I can't stand the cold no more,
'Cause if I ain't livin' to my purpose
Than what am I livin' for!

See, the truth is,

No matter what shape form or fashion it's been,
I've always been on a cycle; in a cycle,
All along it's been me n' only me,
That can control n' determine just how vicious it'll be.
I gotta change this cycle myself,
Recycle myself,
Cause this life is detrimental to my health,
getting older & I still don't know what to do with myself,

Artist, poet n' all of that,
N' the teen in me still yearns to be a running back,
I'm tryin' to find my true calling,
But it's like I'm climbing a glacier n' I keep fallin',
Tryin' to turn my engine over but I keep stallin',
I'm tired of beatin' my head against walls
It's time to enter a new era in my life,
It's time to take flight, choose my directions,
go left or go right,
Whatsoever I choose it better be right,
I'm hungry to fulfill my destiny's appetite,
Gotta stop nibblin' @ the finer things
Go 'head n' take a bite,
Time to walk out of darkness into the glorious light,
Cause if I'm gonna feel the glow I gotta escape the night,
Cause my future is bright. AMEN.
A man's gift will make room for him,
And bring him before great men,
Whether it be 8, 10, or 28 men,
No matter how small or great it is,
There is room n' my gift will make a way in,
N' once I'm in, this is the cycle I wanna stay in,
No more addiction, no more playin', no more delayin'.
It's time to be free.

I wanna be free.
I long to be free.
I wanna be free like a melody playin' in the wind,
I wanna burn myself to a blank CD n' let it spin.
Let it hum sweet serenity into my life.
Smooth, sweet, n' delicious.
Smooth, sweet, n' no longer vicious.

ADO LES CENTS

As a teen I tried to fit in but there wasn't any room,
I was consumed with gloom,
Darkness loomed n' I carried a bad moon,
Got unglued n' subdued,
N' felt like I was livin' in a tomb.

Life was hard n' hectic,
N' I couldn't accept it,
I was gonna flush myself out with antiseptic,
Cause I felt like I was septic,
n' all I did was accept it.

Self-conscious ate away at me day to day,
N' cut away at me weekly,
Like cutlery it cut away at me deeply,
Couldn't bandage it up,
So I just let it bleed away freely.

I should've been on top;
One of the best then.
But I look back at all the classes I dropped n' slept in,
walked out n' left n' all the classes I got n' "F" in,

All of life's dog mess that I stepped in,
I been in n' outta a lot of messes,
Endured a lot of stress,
N' did a lot of 2nd guessin',
It was so hard to figure out n' I felt spent!
n' not on purpose!
Unless it, was all meant,
To add up to a purpose,
But I guess it's just the essence of adolescence,
It all adds up to less cents n' less sense.
But they call it adolescence
cause we add up all the lessons that we learn,
All the lessons that led up to
where we are from where we were,
All the experience learned n' earned,
Stretch marks on my conscious burned,
Growin' is hard n' growin' is stern,
But through it all a man I turned, into;
From all that I've been through,
n' where I've come to,
As I continue to learn n' grow,
There's more that this life has to show,
More things to know, more places to go.
I'm glad I didn't take my life n' blow it,
But rather took the time to grow it.

EVALUATE

What coulda been never was
Cause I didn't take
the time to work at it!
N' that ain't wussup!

But it's real talk.
N' ain't nobody else to blame
there's only 1 cause!
Ain't nobody else to blame
it's all my fault!
I brought a lot of crap all on myself,
So I ought ta' fix it all myself,
I put it all upon myself!
I coulda lost it but I caught it myself!

I got by with a lil'
help from my friends,
Got high wit a lil'
help from my friends,
All the friends that I thought
Were my friends
Who weren't my friends,
Friends don't hurt their friends.
Daddy told me birds
of a feather flock 2gthr!
Son you gotta hang
with people who are headed
to places that you wanna go!
A pastor taught me about friends
a long time ago, he said,
"You can tell your real friends from your fake friends

cause real friends stick with you through thick n' thin,
and you can tell the fake ones
cause when times get thick, they *thin* out!"

Skinny thin friends took a toll,
But I can't blame everybody else
for the state of my life as a whole!
Earthlings don't own my soul!
It's my life, my reigns I hold,
The ways I choose to respond;
Only I control!
A lot of my downfalls n' mistakes
we're self-imposed!
I dug my own potholes!
It's time take all of that crap
N' flush it down a bowl!
It's been wreaking too long,
n' it's straight up old!

I'm ready to join the fold
of those who roll n' stroll down
better paths n' better roads!
Regardless of what anybody thinks,
n' whatever anybody's told,
I know when God made Me,
He broke the mold!

I got so much callin' on me!
Like God's wringin' the
Clouds in the sky,
It's all fallin' on me!
That's why I'm givin' my all to
Be all that I wanna be!

I got a new attitude to suit my aptitude
N' I'm fueled up to reach a higher altitude!
Chances I nearly took that nearly blew away,
Nearly drove themselves to
Detroit Metro in a new blue escape,
n' nearly flew away in a new blue cape,
Like they were lookin' for new a place to escape,
I got work to do n' much to do
I make much ado I got a lot to evaluate,
N' now's my moment what's the use to wait?
There's a world I have to change,
a chance I have to take,
I'm usin' *now* to create somethin'
of value before it's past too late,
No time for truancy like "Hey pal, you late!"
I got a life n' a legacy I have to make,
Got loose ends to amputate,
My goals to go bigger than bantamweight,
There's a lot of moves I have to make;
Calculate n' tabulate every step I have to take,
There may be rules I have to break,
But at any rate I ain't tryin' to
arrive at just any fate or place!
It's time to evacuate n' go after
it now before it evaporates,
Can't let it superannuate, my value's great
n' I have too much at stake!!

I got so much callin' on me!
Like God's wringin' the clouds in the sky,
n' it's all fallin' on me!
That's why I'm givin' my all to
be all that I wanna be!

FACIN' IT

My dirty ass in the shower,
Washin' a weeks worth a' dirt off me!!
Dry off n' brush my teeth
In the mirror lookin' at what my
life work has cost me,
See my Facebook "friends";
They all ballin' out n' I'm stallin' out!
My image cloudy on the glass,
Hard to see a bigger picture,
Hard to draw it out!
But since the mirror's nice n' steamy
Lemme scrawl it out!
I painted myself into a malfunctioning
Self-pitying self-destructing disaster,
Can't get right;
can't get my ass straight,
So I went ass backwards!
Slower forward, faster backwards!
I had it mastered!
My sorry ass crashed,
burned n' shattered!
Breakin' down cryin' to
My mama's pastor probably thinkin' what's
wrong with this sorry bastard!
Take the Good Book n' start
readin' some chapters!
So I did; better yet I do!
I'm tryin' ta' better myself,
not to be better than you,
I'm tryin' ta' be a better ME
cause it's the better thing ta' do!

Tired of buttin my head on the same rock
stuck up in the same spot,
tryin' to break loose but the cage is locked!

Hard to feel uncaged when you're agoraphobic.
Walk around hopin' know one knows it,
No one'll see it or, uh…notice that you're a "phobic."
Between a rock n' a hard place n' you know it,
A rollin' stone gathers no moss; But you ain't rollin'!
Just growing more mold n'
the more you sit, you grow more sick!
You laid out, cried your eyes out, n' hoped
the floor would absorb it.
Don't answer for a person at the door
or who they at the door with!
Can't face the world no more or have
to deal with anymore of this!
For sure you're bored with it,
You're out of orbit n' you can't take anymore of it!
Gotta grow quick;
You can live up or quit, get up or forfeit, it's your pick!
So much to live for but you can't keep ignorin' it!

Perfect flaws in a perfect plan,
My circumstance ain't perfect man,
I try but it ain't workin' man,
My future ain't too certain and
I try to see it in the mirror but it's blurrin' man,
Perhaps perchance I'll get a perfect glance
if I take a certain stance.
Clearly I understand my life is more than worth a damn,
It's in a pair of perfect hands,
Me and the Father holdin' hands,

N' I understand I'll never be a perfect man,
But I'm worth the work for the worth I am.
In my past people made me feel worthless, not worth a *damn*,
I still see it all, *Total Recall*, memories resurface; *damn*.

Your ex didn't believe in you,
Said your dream was unachievable,
It simply wasn't feasible,
Dropped you like a bad habit,
She no longer need ya' bro,
But you got somethin' special,
baby girl just didn't see it though,
It's all about believin' bro,
So you better believe it bro,
It's all about believin' n' achievin' so get believin'
cause you can be UNBELIEVABLE!!!!
Achieve the inconceivable even though
the past has seemed so bleak and low an times when
you felt weak and slow, it's all perceivable,
If you can percieve it you can be it,
But you just gotta see it though!

You can't be yourself if you can't see yourself,
Can't achieve if you don't believe in yourself,
Just to breathe is a gift in an of itself,
Breathe. Believe. Achieve; See Yourself.

Mirror Mirror on the wall; Everyday I'm sayin' it!
I see myself everyday in it!
When I'm facin' it I'm basing it on
makin' it out this basement quick.
Takin' it elevatin' it, raising it above the *basicness*!
I got a destiny n' ain't no escapin' it,

Can't let my dream escape my grip, get away n' split,
So I'm gonna keep chasin' it, embracin' it,
I'm on a path n' I'm gonna stay with it.

I'm in the mirror makin' faces man,
I stand naked before the faceless man
Like damn man here I am again man!
A faceless man, I can't take this man,
But I know in my heart that I gotta face this man!
Gotta face this man in the mirror,
It ain't rocket science it's real basic man!
If you ain't likin' the reflection
then you gotta erase and change it man!
Change is here so embrace it man!
Change is here n' I can taste it man!
N' right now it's tastin' like Colgate!
Oh wait!
I see myself through the fog now,
I can locate my face!
It's all comin' 2gthr now!
Oh it's so great!

SHOOTING STARS

I saw a shooting star the other night,
Shootin' ever so high,
Shinin' ever so bright,
I was blinded by the light,
It asked me what I want outta life,
N' whatever I might like,
N' to tell it my dreams,
N' what I see in my sights,

So I opened my mind,
N' closed my eyes ever so tight,
N' I hoped n' wished with all of my might,
N' I took my time,
So I could get it all right before I write;
Alright.

N' pardon this little typo,
Matter-of-fact I saw 2 to my surprise,
In the night blue skies, two blurred in the sky,
A double portion of wishes flew right before my eyes,
That's why every night I glue my eyes to the skies!
Cause I don't wanna miss out on anything,
Ain't no tellin' when the stars are out
what kinda wishes they might bring!
So I replied with this;

I wanna be like you Star.

I just wanna take flight,
Spontaneously combust n' ignite,
N' transmit via satellites!
I wanna travel to far away destinations,
Far away to other lands n' distant nations,
Far away where I can dance with constellations,
To a state of infinite bliss n' constant elations,
Free to seek n' fulfill my will n'
my every temptation, joys n' sensations,
I want it now sooner than later n' I'm tired of waitin'!
I wanna explode like a solar burst,
Like a Big Bang without the Theory,
I wanna streak across the sky!
I wanna go places,

from continent to continent,
N' meet all of the different races,
I wanna be like you Star,
I wanna be celestial,
Orbit all the planets wavin' to extraterrestrials,
I wanna pet white dwarves!
Leave the 3rd Rock from the Sun,
Moonlight on Venus then teleport to Mercury,
Lay out like a solar panel and absorb the power of ten suns!
Change my name to Edmond and fly with Halley like;
See ya' in 2061!!
Come back and circle the moon 20 times
n' make it back to Houston without a problem!

I wanna travel upward to infinity n' light years beyond
the furthest reaches on a starship voyage,
Be transported thru blackholes into other dimensions,
Be hurled thru Andromedas n' take
Quantum Leaps past quasars
N' emerge on the other side of
Stargates like a Starship Trooper!
I wanna go further than the Final Frontier;
Where no man has gone before!
I wanna feel the power of the force!

I wanna be like you in every way.
I wish to be bound by nothing.
No longer bound by laws or principalities,
No longer bound by time, strung out on a line,
I'll put time in a bind, tie it in a bow,
Escort it Back II the Future and present it to
an alternate version of myself in an
alternate universe and re-write it.

And just for kicks, no pun intended,
I'll kick Biff in his nuts before I take off
with Marty in Doc's DeLorean!
Take McFly back to 1985,
Leave 'Then', come back to 'Today',
then blast away into the Life of Tomorrow!

N' even though I may be in another stratosphere
Far above the hemisphere,
I still wanna be near to *here*,
Livin' on a high level n' yet still anchored
to my fellow earthlings and elevate others.
My connections;
Ain't no such place as "Too Far",
Ain't no such thing as "Tryin' too hard!"
But I can't be too far from where my few are,
They my connections,
Don't wanna go too far.
Wanna be sure they have more than 2 bars,
Of my reception, can't lose our connection,
Wanna stay more close,
to those I pray for most,
So I can share my blessin's,
Star!!

I wish and pray that you keep me Teflon'd from hater types,
Cause haters gripe, like to dislike, lay off in the cut n' snipe,
The New Year's types,
Who get hype n' bust their pipes into the night,
Aiming, n' *shooting* stars!
Keep me outta reach of the flare of their firearms,
Alert me loudly like the blare of a fire alarm!
N' not only me,

Keep my loved ones from a hater's harm.
God. Star. Star God. God Star.
Dear God, I wanna be like you, cause you rule the near n' far!
Help me align my time, and my life to the stars.

Dear God, I wanna be like you.
Till' the day I become cosmo-dust,
N' scatter my ashes amongst cosmic debris,
That's the reply, the request, n'
response you gonna get from me.

This ain't no nursery rhyme by far,
No Jiminy Cricket or Cinderella in a horse drawn cart,
But twinkle-twinkle little star,
Always wondered where you were,
But now I know just where you are,
You beat right here within my heart.
So at night when I star gaze when twilight embarks,
I admire the moon,
N' though I wish I could,
I can't quite see way out to Mars,
So I just focus a little closer,
N' keep my eyes on the stars.

Impatience N' Frustration

A stream of disassembled
thoughts race down the assembly
line of my mind, hoping to
find their way into a pair
of capable hands that
can put them back together.
My thoughts shift like Tectonic plates,
Separating the Pangea of my mind.
I've rearranged Egypt, relocated Israel.
Shifted Antarctica.
My thoughts are in a continental shift and I am polarized.
Nearly demoralized, highs and lows,
But I spend more time on my lower side!

Not molar sized it's motor-sized!
A mechanism that's motorized.
I've worn down over time,
Eyes Wide Shut; Lids closed over eyes.
So I blindly trip over my fault-lines.

I'm tryin' to organize my confusion,
Jumpin' to conclusions and landin' on illusions,
Eludin' the truth n' I fight to search my mind
to find solutions, and block out all the noise pollution.

Frustration's building up in me like seismic activity!
Ready to explode outta mental captivity!

I'm full of flaws and faults. My thoughts are
broken up into continents and it's all my fault!
Fault-lines breaking me up into so many pieces

I've run out of solid ground to stand on.
I've plummeted and capsized into arctic waters,
n' I'm nearly drowning trying to swim around
the fragments of Myself.
Strokin' n' floatin n' hopin' till the tides
wash me up to shore, and I arrive at the Island of ME.
I am on The Island of ME.
Fighting to bring it all back together.

One mind,
One thought,
One land mass,
One continent.
And it's hard.
Frustrating.
Testing my patience.

Frustration is my No. 1 aquaintance,
It accompanies me day to day; I can't take it!
I'm caught in a cycle n' I can't break it!
I'm tryin' ta' juke the blues but I can't shake it!
My blues never take a vacation!
Life sucks n' at times
I think I can't make it!
Try ta' cheer myself up but I can't fake it.
They say life is what we make it;
But a mess is how I made it!
Now all I am is frustrated n' runnin' outta patience!

Patience is a virtue,
One among other cliches
That weren't true!
Impatience n' frustration ='s Annoyance!

I'm in a cafeteria lunch line
waitin' for a tray of Clairvoyance
to be served to those who need it most!
N' I need it more than most,
I'll gladly be the recipient n' host
to new clarity cause
It's been such a rarity, it's so rare to me,
I barely possess it n' that's why I stress it,
I wanna get it so bad that it's drivin' me so mad!!
It's somethin' I've hardly known or had.
I'm so sick! I'm so tired! I'm so sick n' tired
of bein' sick n' tired n' tired out!!
Frustrated n' runnin' outta patience!!
Sometimes I still get frustrated with my past,
Like I shoulda' learned more Spanish
n' worked harder @ Math!
Go back n' re-take every test I didn't pass!
Shoulda' stepped up for my Mama
when she was strugglin' to stay a float!!
I'm frustrated with always feelin' like a fish outta water!!
Being a visionary who's caught between two extremes;
Having 'Nothing', wanting 'Everything',
and struggling just to get 'Something'!!

Hell, I almost ran out of patience with this poem,
grew frustrated with the writer's block
that nearly blocked this creation.
Damn, a *Polar Vortex* is swallowing the state
of Michigan and I'm snowed in with writer's block!!!!
Now ain't that lovely!!!!

I'm runnin' out patience with women,
They say nice guys finish last

so I'm frustrated when they don't call like;
Do you know who I am?!!
I may not seem like much at the moment
but you lookin' at a brotha' that's gonna impact
the World, let alone yo' life!!

I'm frustrated by the TV!!
Cause whether or not whatever they're
airing is old or new, to me it's *all* a rerun!!
And all that reflects back to me is that
my very life is a rerun! N' that's frustrating.

I'm impatient and frustrated with my loneliness.
Depression, anxiety, and agoraphobia
have me locked away, n' I can't take it another day,
but I can't break away!
Damn these chains!!
I remain restrained, stranded,
a castaway on an island of ME.
ALONE.
No Wilson, just a comp book of poems, prayers,
and the sound of my own heartbeat.
Somethings are just out of my control.

Pangea.
Tectonic plates.
Continental shift.
Seismic activity.
Can't change the past.
Can't control the weather.
Can't control what other people think or do.

James Allen once wrote;

"Man cannot choose his circumstance,
but he **can** choose his thoughts, and
thus, indirectly, change his circumstance."

and;

"A man becomes calm in the measure that he understands
himself as a thought-evolved being....
and sees more and more clearly the internal relations of
things by the action of cause and effect, he ceases to fuss and
fume and worry and grieve, and remains poised, steadfast,
serene."

I can rearranged my Egypt, relocate my Israel.
Shift my Antarctica.

And as the stream of my disassembled
thoughts race down the assembly
line of my mind, hoping to
find their way into a pair
of capable hands that
can put them back together,
I will realize that the only person I'll see standing
at the end of that line; is ME.

SQUEEZED

I work hard as hell,
It ain't hard to tell,
But many times I work hard n' fail,
I'm workin' hard to prevail,
In this tough world hard as nails,
Waves so rough it's hard to sail,
Hard to climb n' scale.
In all things there's effort n' hard work,
Nothing's ever done with ease,
I hold the tools,
I hold the keys,
Ta' press back against
the struggles that press against ME!
Apply pressure to a lemon n'
you get the juice n' the seeds,
N' I ask myself;
What oozes outta me whenever I'm squeezed?
Doubts, fears, and disbeliefs?
When the forces of nature
Are poundin' on my walls,
Will I walk tall or fall n' crawl?
Will I break down in stall?
Will I stand up n' face it all?
Face it y'all it's basic all there is
to do is whatever it takes ta' make it dogg!
He who is afraid of doing too much
always does too little,
That's why I'm tryin'
ta' whittle as much as I can chisel.

I gotta take claim of my life,

Gotta change my life,
Rearrange my life,
No matter what strains n' pains my life,
I gotta exchange my life;
For another!
Gotta live my life for me,
N' not for another!
No other!
I'm tired of my life bein' under siege,
Life's ready for me ta' seize,
I'm ready n' freshly squeezed!

BACK 2 THE FUTURE

How can you reverse time?
Tell me?
How can you change a mind?
How can you replace years that have been lost?
Enlighten me.
How can you mend a broken man?
Tell me if you can.
For one to learn to live again,
where does on begin?

If I could travel time I'd travel mine,
I would rattle every riddle,
I'd unravel every rhyme,
Find every answer I have to find,
To loose the shackles of my mind,
If I could only press rewind.
To travel time.
To travel mine.

But if I go back I couldn't stay,
For I know I must come back someday.
When I do, what do I do now?
How can I press forward?
Someone tell me how.
How can I sustain myself from day to day?
Have you any suggestions?
Cause I'm hard up and stuck
with no answers to my questions.
How can I rewrite my life anew and
start a fresh new chapter?
How can I make my next move my best move
and all the moves thereafter?

If I could travel time I'd travel mine.
I would rattle every riddle,
I'd unravel every rhyme,
Find every answer I could find,
To loose the shackles of my mind,
If I can press on over the course of time.
To travel time.
To travel mine.
And in the end what will I find?
Will my life be a success or a wasteful grind?
Perhaps it's all intertwined within my mind.

IF, AND, BUT, MAYBE

What *if* I would have wrapped it up or pulled out,
And not have gotten caught up in the feeling?
But would've been thinking
with the head on my shoulders
instead of the one that's 'lower'.
Maybe it would've kept our relationship
from dragging on longer than it did.
Maybe I should'a went
back to Ohio after she dumped me,
I could'a been a free bachelor,
free to do and live as I pleased.
Perhaps I would'a been better off
and happier back home.

What *if* I actually would have paid attention
in class and did all of my homework,
And didn't get suspended all the time and serve
a thousand detentions?
But showed up on time and didn't get in fights.
Maybe if I didn't just wanna hit up parties and get
drunk and high I might have been more.
I should'a had my priorities straight,
and *maybe* I could'a stayed
eligible to play for the Cardinals,
and got a scholarship to play ball,
or *maybe* I could'a got a
full-ride to one of the most prestigious
art institutions in the nation.
Maybe I would'a been like J.Scott Campbell,
or animating at Disney Pixar.

What *if* I would have been smarter about it all,
And watched who I dealt and served to?
But would have been more protective and selective,
Maybe, oh *maybe*, I wouldn't have got popped
n' everything could have been different.
I should'a remembered the
traps that Dad told me about,
the dangers and the consequences,
I could'a spared myself a lot of trouble and grief,
n' I would'a never got myself
involved in that life in the first place.

In life there are no *SHOULD'A, COULD'A, WOULD'As.*
No I *SHOULD'A*, an if I *COULD'A* I *WOULD'A.*
It is what it is.
I tried what I could and did what I did.
There is no Butterfly Effect that
can be evoked in any scenario,
No Ashton Kutcher to manifest
himself like a State Farm
insurance agent, equipped with a
magical comp-book endowed
with the power to majestically transport us
to a moment in our past to reconstruct moments
and repair the things in life that went askew.
I can't go back to 1997, 2001, or 2010,
and neither can you.

A man once told me that in life
we don't get 'Do Overs",
We get 'Do Betters'.
There's the saying, 'If I knew then what I know now.'
There's nothing we can do to rectify the past,

No 'Do Overs', only 'Do Betters'.
So hey, I may not have known it then,
but I know now.
So if I get a second chance, all I can do is take what
I know now, and I better do it BETTER.

I'm blessed by the dumb stuff I've done.
And I would do *everything'* in my power,
not to change a thing.
What some may see as a mistake,
is really a blessing in disguise.
No child is a mistake.
Blessed was the day that my
beautiful daughter entered this world.
I wouldn't change that for anything.
She completes me.
She is my world and I would be
lost in this world without her
beautiful smile, her infectious laugh,
and her playful heart.
When I look into her eyes I see the future,
I see evolution,
I see a great destiny to be realized,
a prophecy to someday be fulfilled.

Oh yes I have struggled, and
I've learned from my struggle;
where would I be without it?
I've learned from mistakes I've made,
in times when I didn't know,
n' I still don't know everything,
but life is a journey and a process,
and I'm just trying to grow.

I have no regrets.
What was, simply *was*.
What is to be, must be.
There are no SHOULDA, COULDA,
WOULDAs that can change it.
There are no IF's, no AND's, no BUT's, and no MAYBE's.

SHORT STUFF

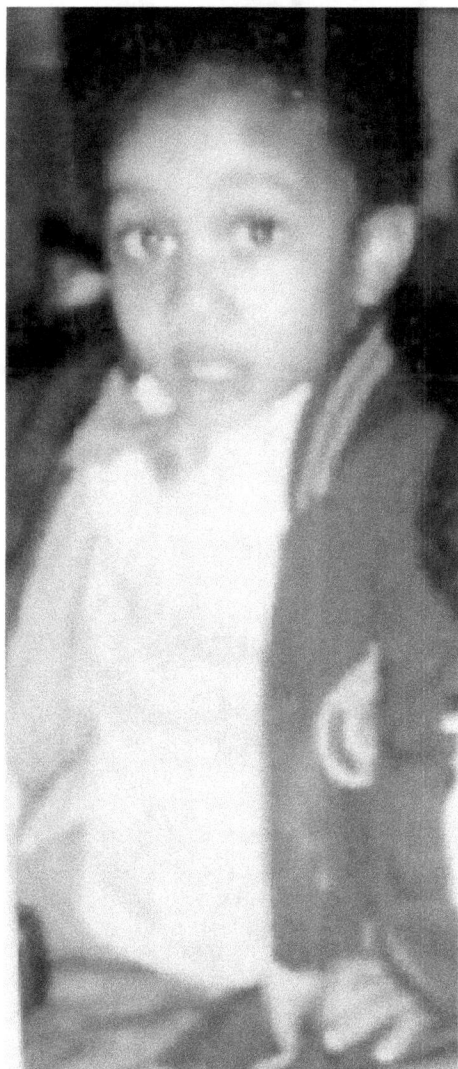

OVERSHADOWED

The world has grown so tall around me;
Redwood like.
And I, the extraterrestrial,
shuffle in the shadows beneath.

PEDESTRIAN

Don't wanna take leisurely strolls
through yesterdays,
The thought is dreadful in
the back of my mind,
I've been back in time,
Come and gone again and again,
Around and around,
I've been to where the sidewalk ends.

HANGMAN

I'm suspended in animation.
Dangling at the end of a rope
that's held by a laughing lunatic
who's holding a pair of scissors!
Lord, still his hands,
Rescue me before the twine is sheared.

ILLEISM

In the mirror you see *yourself.*
You hear *yourself.*
But it is not *you.*
For somebody else has
Taken *your* place.
Backstabber laughing in *your* face,
Illeism is his name,
Laughing, pointing back at you like; *'IN YO' FACE!'*

QUIETTIME

Quiet!
Pipe down in there!
Shut up n' stop thinking!
Cause when you think you overthink,
N' when you overthink,
You do things without thinking!

E-TOXIFY

I suffer withdrawals from
the happiness of another life,
Phening to be clean,
I yearn the true fix.

...IS 20/20

Too soon old,
Too late wise,
Life, viewed in reverse.
Hindsight can be far too often.

TOXIC SURPLUS

Carbon dioxide on the inhalation,
Sulfur in the exhale.
Gas masks imperative; none at my disposal.
Breathing tubes and CO_2 tanks; Readily available.

sQUAREDANCING

I feel like I'm sQuare dancing my way through life!
1 step forward then 3 steps back,
2 to the side then a lil' do-see-doe!
N' I just find myself right back
at the same position I was in when I started.

TIMELINE

Where have I been?
Where have I gone?
Where am I going?
God knows how long it'll be 'till
I break through to the other side.
The next stage of this timeline.
What have I done, what'll I do?

Don't know what's in this life for me,
But this much is true,
I gotta make moves, I gotta move on,
There's a timeline for everyone I'm not the only one.

Things that I've dreamed,
Things that I've seen,
Things that I'll see and it seems,
That this world is mine and it was made for me,
So wherever I go and whatever I see,
Whatever I do I know this much is true,
I gotta make moves.
I gotta move on.
There's a timeline for everyone,
Gotta make moves,
Before my time is done.

WELCOME BACK HARPER

"I YEARS HAD BEEN FROM HOME." - EMILY DICKINSON

"Welcome back Harper!
You turned out swell,
You've come such a long way
And you're doing so well!"

Yeah right!
Take a snapshot of my life,
The picture's out of focus.
My life ain't right,
I'm just a hot mess who can't sleep at night!

So *welcome back* whatever!
At times I feel as if I'm just too far gone!

I, regurgitated from the past,
Won't return to a parade in my honor,
No streets will be named to commemorate me,
No key to the city.
Just a quiet hope,
That someone has missed me.

EMPTY HANDED

"MAN IS A GROWTH BY LAW" - JAMES ALLEN

Not what I want and yearn for will I get,
But only what I earn.
Nothin' from nothin' leaves nothin',
I get what I deserve,
And keep coming back for more.

REVOLUTIONS

Calmly the world revolves,
It's subjects whiz in frantic circles,
Outside of the circles am I,
Content with revolving *with* the world,
Rather than it spinning hectically,
Around me.

JUGGLIST

As I juggle the struggle from one day to another,
I fumble and stumble,
Life's got me by the jugular,
Life is brutal and punishing.

I won't let it get to me,
I keep going and growing stronger,
This road is long but I can run a little longer,
Maybe the world I can conquer!

I insist to persist, constantly vigorous,
And always relentless,
Cause I'm built for this,
I'm Neo in this Matrix,
Armed with sledgehammer,
I'm 'bout to break this!
I believe this,
I dream this,
I know I can achieve this,
And one day I'm gonna see this,
I breathe this.
I juggle the struggle like a jugglist.

ALL THE WHILE, JUST THE SAME

I have held solace,
I have traveled side by side with burdens,
All the while; *incomplete* just the same,
As an ocean without tides.

I have feasted on the fat of the land,
I have scrapped the feeble morsels of the Earth,
All the while; *empty* just the same,
As a vacant dwelling.

I have discovered; *EUREKA!*
I have dug empty wells,
All the while; *searching* just the same,
As a lonesome dove gone astray.

THE BEATDOWN

It's a sad sight for sore eyes
To see a grown man cry,
N' I'm a grown man cryin',
A grown man tryin' but I'm dyin',
When I lay me down to sleep,
A death bed is what I lie in.

My life is in a bad mess,
I'm a walkin' talkin' poet
Writtin' nothin' but sadness,
and takin' some bad hits.
Fightin' a losin' battle n'
gettin' my tail kicked!
I get my tail whipped at
every turn I take,
Fallin' apart at the seams,
It seems I'm about to break!
Don't know how much more I can take,
I'm livin' in a bad dream,
N' the whole time I'm wide awake!

GOD IS IN THE RAIN

Despite all of my shortcomings,
Despite all of my pain,
I find solace in the notion that God is in the rain.

Wash me.
Wash me clean of the world's foul stench,
A sprinkle will not suffice,
Lord I wanna get drenched,
Until my thirsty void has been quenched.

Cleanse me.
Cleanse doubt from my mind,
And fear from my heart,
Replenish me with strength and wisdom,
Till death do me part.

Purge me.
Purge me of the sicknesses that I've identified,
Through you & only you can the antidote be supplied,
Sanitize my aliments one by one,
May they be swept away by the tide.

To each life some rain must fall,
So I'm thankful for the rainy days,
I'm thankful for them all.
For they purge and wash away my pain,
Cleanse my soul of all life's stains,
I'm thankful for the perspective I've gained,
I find solace in knowing;
That God is in the rain.

PRO-LIFE

Impregnated with choices.
Hopes.
Dreams.
Doubt, is a contraceptive
fighting to intervene.
My dream is a seed I cannot abort.

FEEL

Have you ever felt?
Do you know how it feels?
I guess what I'm really askin' is,
Have you ever really felt anything?

There was a time when I didn't feel anything at all.
I felt nothing.
My emotions were anesthetized.
Until someone named poetry came along.

I use this poetry.
Abuse this poetry.
It's my performance enhancing drug.

I can close my eyes....
and just feel.

FATHER OF MINE

For years I let anger and
resentment well up inside,
But over the years I've learned to set it aside,
For to err is human, to forgive is divine,
May God renew your spirit and
May God renew your mind, as well as mine.
Peace of mind we can find, I love you.
Father of mine.

LOOKING the

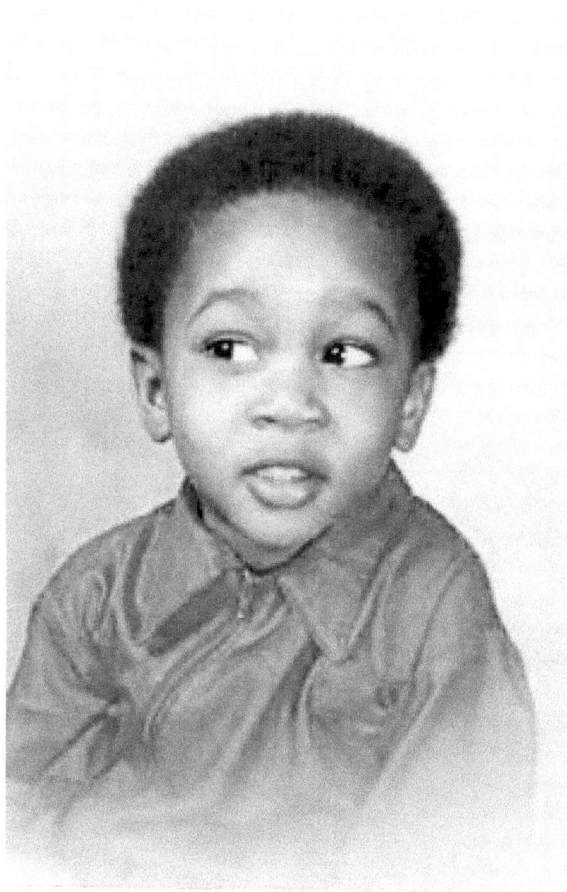

OTHER WAY

SEEIN' ME

@ times I find my eyes in a far gaze far away,
I sit back n' I star gaze, farther than Mars,
Tryin' ta' see past all'a my hard days,
Confused jarred n' dazed.
N' I see myself in a whole other galaxy,
In a whole other universe where I'm
No longer just eMajining fantasies,
I'll no longer be battling with my mind scattering,
N' no vices'll rattle me,
Oh how wonderful that'll be!
But in the meantime I'm in between grinds
n' I gotta handle reality.

It's hard @ times ta' wrap my mind
around everything that's goin' on,
My life's been out of alignment
so long, *everything's* goin' wrong!

Dolla's burned in my palms whenever I held em',
Me flossin' n' tossin' money; very seldom,
I never go to the mall cause I never feel welcomed.
By the time I get there every $ is spent
I dig into my pockets n' pull out a' wad'a lint!

I hate pullin' into an ATM,
I got more digits in my pin,
Then my actual dividends!
You say 'what about divids' friends?
I'll laugh and say my 'divids' END!!
This is factual, I ain't kiddin' friends,
I struggle ta' get my ends,

BRIAN HARPER 93

I work ta' make bread, I just wanna get ahead,
Get the stress off'a my head,
You can wish me good luck,
But I ain't gonna break a leg!

Can't support nobody else, can't support myself!
My money's shorter than a Keebler Elf!
I'm a crappy supporter!
Can't do nothin' for my daughter
I can't even support er',
She need new clothes n' I can't even afford em'!
It's makes me wanna jump off of a bridge
n' smack my head on some water!
I'm dyin' inside, n' I can feel my breath gettin' shorter!!
My pride ain't soarin', my pride is sore
n' it's growin' shorter n' shorter,
I feel like a midget of a man,
I can't take it no more n' my credit sucks,
I rob Peter to pay Paul before I pay Al,
Hey Sal, wire me some money from PayPal!
Hustle everyday tryin ta make a piece of money,
Tryin' ta' feed the seed off a' pizza money!

I remember;
I've worked 14 different jobs in the last four years,
23 all together since I moved here to MI in 2001,
I've had 16 different address,
15 if you take away the few
months that I slept in my Taurus.

Life's been suckin' blah through a straw,
One *"sidedly"* disappointin'.
I know I'm goin' off right now

but I ain't holdin' back what I'm feelin',
I spill it when I feel it n' till I'm finished,
I'm spillin' nuthin' but buckets of realness!
Illness, stuff that I don't even wanna deal with!
I'm so stressed, I can't even finish a meal.

This crap's gonna send me off the deep end **real quick!**

REAL TALK;
I've attended hotel conventions
where they tell you can change ya' life!
Change ya' job,
Change ya' friends,
n' change ya' wife!
Ya' family n' friends'll
Be estranged for life!
You can even leave the convention
n' get some strange tonite!

Buy a vendin' machine; **Be a millionaire!**
Sell Monavie!
Leave ya' old job like a distinguished honoree!
This is so cute, I'ma be filthy rich!
Sportin' new suits n' sellin' fruit juice?!!
That's funny like a dentist with a tooth loose!
I'll be dang!
I was born @ night, but not last night!
And that's all I gotta say.
Only dreams come to sleepers,
only hard work pays.
I'm workin' to live mine while I'm awake!
I'm workin so hard everyday,

I'm Goin so hard everyday,
I'm goin' so 'No Holds Barred' at this dream,
EVERYDAY!!

I dream as if I'll live forever, I live as if I'll die today.
Cause I ain't got nothin' but a Dream,
n' a gleam glowin' like a bright beam.

I created the fire, n' I choked on the smoke,
But gettin' shook couldn't shake me,
Bad breaks couldn't break me!
N' now I'ma do whatever it takes for me to make the life I
wanna make,
Give it all that it takes, and take all the takes I can take,
For however long it takes me!

Gotta use the past as fertilizer, to nourish my change.

Cause my life's outta order,
I gotta REARRANGE!!
I'm gonna be the change,
I can see the change!

Have confidence an I can accomplish it.

O' say I can see!

I can see that ME!
With everything I want
n' everything I need!
Doin' what I want n' bein' all the things I wanna be!
Yeah I can see em',
I keep believin', n' one day I'm gonna be em'!

I can see that ME,
I wanna be that ME!!
N' God as my witness, *I'm gonna BE that ME!*

Despite everything in ME life,
Everything'll be right,
Everything'll be tight,
God's got a plan for how everything'll be like.

Ask me how I know; *I CAN SEE IT.*

DOO DOO

My job is a reflection of my life,
Doing what everybody else wants me to do,
Never what I wanna do,
Always stuff I don't wanna do,
Somebody's always asking me to do somethin' I
Don't wanna do,
"Do you wanna do something for me?"
I really wanna say no,
But it's my job, I'm getting paid,
So I just let it go.
Even though I don't wanna do it though.
I have a mountain of things that I have to do,
But don't really wanna do,
And I have 8 hours to do them,
I start off with the 1st thing I have to do,
the 1st thing I don't wanna do
Because now's the best time to do it,
Even though it's something I really don't wanna do,
But I can't even do that which I'm doing,

Because someone else is asking me to
do something else that I don't want to do,
on top of what I already don't wanna do,
So what am I to do?
I haven't got a clue,
I've asked myself a million times
and now I'm asking you.
I'm tired of not doing nothing for myself,
All of this not-doing can't be good for my health,
So what I'll do is look within,
to search for what is true,
And then perhaps,
Perhaps just then,
I'll know just what to do.

I've swallowed a jagged pill a thousand times,
I'm regurgitating blood in puddles of disgust n' discontent!
This can't be the way work was meant!
I don't come to work for this!
A man should enjoy his work n' his craft,
N' feel fulfilled after bustin' his ass!
Buildin' somethin' he can cherish n' somethin' that'll last!
Not just workin' for some cash,
But livin' ta' have a blast!
It hurts wakin' up in the mornin',
my mind n' my body achin' n' sore,
N' my confidence isn't soarin',
My ADL's are freakin' borin',
My cup got a leak in it,
So it isn't pourin'; OVER!
I've had it up to hear,
I'm sayin' NO MORE!!
N' this can't be what it's all about,

There's gotta be somethin' more n' this can't be
what life is for when I'm s'posed to blessed
n' *Just Doin' It* like Michael Jordan!
Lookin' for opportunity but I can't find n' open door
n' I'm down on my knees on the floor
n' prayin' askin' what's this all about,
I'm full a' so much a doubt,
I'm in need of a lil' guidance Lord just help me figure it out!

This shit is DOO-DOO!!

Instead of bein' occupied n' killin' time I waste mine!
N' most of the time I feel like time's killin' ME!
DEATH AT THE HANDS OF TIME!!

I spend 8 hrs of my day,
5 days of my week bustin' my hump doin' work for others,
Poetry is what I do for me!
Tired of people complainin'
on me defiling my name,
The rear of my shirt blood soaked from
all the knives I extract out my back!
My life's a train wreck!
My brain's wrecked!
My existence is a gory crime scene on the same set!
It all remains the same except;
NCIS ain't cleaned up the stains yet!

God forbid I clock in 2 min early!
God forbid I clock in 2 min late!
God forbid I get hurt n' break my leg by mistake!
God forbids I get the runs so bad I make my plunger break!
I got a headache n' I'm nauseous!

BRIAN HARPER 99

Don't feel good but I better be cautious!
If I call in again it'll upset my bosses!

This junk is DOO DOO!!
I'ma DOO DOO all over this place!!

What can I DOO DOO for you?!!
Let's see!
I can DOO DOO a lot but I won't do it for free!

What you gonna DOO DOO for me?!!
Not much?! O' I see!!
Well I guess it's BOO-HOO for YOU!! I'm out!!
Baby I gotta DOO DOO for ME!!

MORTHNNEQL2

I'm More than...
Greater and lesser than...
And equal to all 7 billion persons
that inhabit this planet.

Gifted beyond measure,
Faulty by many means,
n' it's ALL good in
the greater scheme of things.
Less than reality n'
more than a dream.
Less than inside the margins,
N' more beyond the seams.
I'm less than what you of think of me,
N' yet I'm more than it seems!

Cause; I'm greater than lesser than
n' all that's in between.
Greater than lesser than n'
equal too; plus him, her, this,
or that n' that Equals you!

I'm greater than any plus or minus,
N' more than any dividend,
Life cannot subtract anything
from the equation of ME
without adding something else
To refill the void!
All things come in due season,
for whatever particular reason.
I'll keep preparin' to recieve em',
n' keep believin' as
long as I'm breathin' that
everything'll balance out n' be even;
Cause I'm greater than
lesser than n' equal to
any form of matter that gathers.
I am nothing more or nothing less.
I'm more than my failures
n' more than my success.
I'm greater than my highs n' lows,
N' I 8nt perfect but I'm quite sure that
my cons are lesser than my pros.

I co-exist with greatness,
Split time with indifference,
and stride side by side with equality.
There is a balance in ALL things.
N' since I'm greater than lesser than

N' equal to all of you;
Just get your mind right baby, cause you are too!

REPENT: Make a Deposit for Change

Allow me to tell you what brings me in here today.
I'm in need of a new line of credit,
N' I'm in need of a new loan
for a little extra mercy n' grace,
N' some forgiveness.
I've gone over all the checks n' balances,
N' after checkin' myself I've found that
Things just aren't balancing out.
I gotta make a swift withdrawal,
I've invested too much into a non-mutual fund,
I wanna start a new life savings,
I've spent a lifetime banking on the wrong stocks,
N' my bonds are of no value.
I've been taxed heavily by the burden of guilt n' sorrow,
n' the interest rate is high today,
But it'll be even higher tomorrow,
N' I feel as if I've run outta grace n' mercy to borrow.
My assets have depleted,
I've foreclosed n' forfeited all of what I bared in my name.
My consultants have run out of options for me,
N' Chapter 11 has presented itself as my last resort.
I'm ready to pay my debts,
and put my past behind me n' start over fresh.
So I'm here today to fill out n' sign some new paperwork,
I'm here to make a new investment,
to open a new account,

n' to make a deposit for change,
Cause there's some things in my life,
That I simply have to change.

A PRAYER FROM THE BACKSEAT

We don't get out of life what we want,
We get out of life who we are.
Who am I?
Out here all alone.
Who am I?
Out here on my own.
Who am I?
Alone on my own without a
home to call my own.

I've been living my life from the backseat.
My will is in the backseat,
My heart is on the floor board,
and my dreams are in the trunk.
No one's a real friend,
I'm friends with my pens,
Pen pals.

Your really far away from home
when you ain't got one.
I can't think straight sometimes.
I've been doin things I shouldn't do.
I'm livin in this crap.
I'm breathing in my nightmares,
exhalin' my terrors,
My breath clinging to my windshield,

As far as Eye can see, I see no hope for *me*.

Urinating in hollow bottles,
Searching for a place to hide,
My safe haven is my ride.
My Backseat, my bed.
My Storage unit, my attic.
My trunk is my closet,
An abandoned truck loading dock; My Bat Cave.
I'm sleeping on a couch;
Wherever I can find one,
A deserted parking lot;
Wherever I can find one.
Staying on my boss's couch,
In my co-worker's trailer, or back to
my driver's seat; Reclining/Declining.
My life is declining n' I don't wanna fall back too far.
I'm curled up, messed my world up
with bad decisions.
I'm tired of beatin' my brain against a table,
When I know I'm able, to write my life; no fable.
My mind's a labyrinth
and I'm scattered in it, shattered in it .
For so long I've gone to bed with my truth,
only to wake up to my lies.

And now I wake up in a sedan; my home on wheels.
My new apartment, my condo, my townhouse,
My mansion, my casa. My Bed.

Too ashamed to tell my Mama in Ohio,
She ask me how I'm doin' but I lie though,
Say I'm doin' fine, taking it one day at time.

I just wanna spare her from the worry and grief.
She's given her all for me, and she'll do it at
the drop of a dime. I just don't wanna cost her
anything more; money or time.
She's not responsible for cleaning up my mess,
I'm a grown man, n' this burden is mine.

So low, so unstable, I'm unable to provide.
That sweet child of mine.
That sweet child of mine, I have no place for
her that she can call 'Daddy's'.
All I can offer her are potholes n' puddles.
Barbed-wired fences and street lights.
Kids make play of puddles,
But I can't make play of *this*.

Burdened and Lonely.
Single and it's *real* hard to mingle.
Can't imagine entertaining guests in here.
Listening to the Pistons and Red Wings in here.
And oh, what a nice way to meet and court a young lady,
what a perfect way to woo a shorty, huh?
Cause *all* the chicks swoon over the homeless
pizza delivery guy right?

Like hey mama, how'd you like to spend
the night with me in a 2005 Ford Taurus huh?
We can dial through the radio stations
and tune in to ourselves,
lay back the seats or just jump straight to back and
create a Quiet Storm of our own!
We can make *sweet, sweet, love.*
Every window will be fogged with our passion,

and we'll wipe away that mist,
Gaze at the stars through the windshield
like it's the Hubble Telescope,
and the moon's glow will blanket us both.
Then we can cozy up in front of the heat vents
for 10 minute intervals (to preserve my gas, ya' know?).
Our body heat can be our anti-freeze.
We'll converse and burn the midnight oil,
Share an 8 corner and our insecurities.
Then secure and reassure one another.
We'll speak about life, a home, children.
Buckeyes vs. Wolverines.
We'll pick out our marriage venue,
our reception and honeymoon locations,
Set it all in stone like; *BET!!*
All before the sun crawls out of bed.
Then I'll crank it, reverse outta this spot, throw it in drive
n' we'll cruise off into our future.
Oh yeah, I can win her heart with that right?
That's exactly how the scenario'll play out right?
If only in a perfect world, with a perfect girl.
But see I'm earthbound and buckled up in the
realm of reality and I'm LONELY as HELL!!

I awake from my Nicholas Sparks directed dreams.
Situation bleak, can't leave the car runnin' so I sleep
without a lover and without heat,
I'm freakin' cold n' my teeth clink,
ain't had a decent peep of sleep for six weeks,
No toilet to take a leak, I can't cook I can't eat,
Nobody to talk to so I just speak or lip sync,
eyelids heavy but I can't blink,
I try to process my thoughts but I can't think!

Prayin' in the backseat!!
Someone's in the backseat! I'm an Urban Legend.
Someone's in the backseat!
Someone's in the backseat; and it's Me.
Someone's crying in the backseat.
Hurting in the backseat.
Hoping and wishing in the backseat.
Someone's lonely in the backseat, and nobody sees.
Someone's praying in the backseat; and it's Me.
Can you hear me Lord?

Our Father which art in heaven, hollow be my life,
my stomach rumbles for your daily bread.
This is my prayer from the backseat,
I have a prayer and I've been trying to get it to You.
I sleep with a Bible underneath my pillow.
Jesus take the wheel, my life is packed in here!
Drive me far away, clear from here,
I don't know where I should go
That's why I'm trusting you to steer.
I pray for a smoother ride.
Be my ignition.
I'm off balance, I need a realignment,
a rotation, a recalibration.
Fill the reservoir of my depleted spirit
and reset my gauges.
Men do not attract that which they want,
*but that which they **are.*** Who am I?
Lord knows I'm more than this;
I know I'm more than this.
N' I know I've made the bed that I lay in,
but it ain't the bed I wanna stay in,
All I'm sayin' n' relayin' is I ain't got

no time for playin or delayin,
when I'm layin in the backseat prayin'.
Tryin' to convince myself that
I'm getting closer to my dreams,
but at times I believe I'm drifting further away it seems.
Lord I know that if I take your hand
You will hold mine the whole
way through and never let go.
I'm praying right where I'm at.
Take me where I wanna be, to the life I wanna see,
I can't change the world living in the backseat.
Lord give me the heart of a lion
and the strength of ten men.
Laser sharp focus, the serenity of a Buddhist,
the clarity and clairvoyance of a median.
I am the new stone that the builders refused,
Lord make me the Head Cornerstone.
Unbuckle me from this life.
You take the wheel, and I'll ride with you.
Drive me. Be my ride. Be my guide. Be my drive.
I can't make it on my own.
I'm trusting in you to make a way,
and I'm believing that you already have.

HOLD ON TOLETGO @ *30 yrs old*

Don't know why I've been holdin' on so long for,
I don't understand and I just don't know,
Guess I've been holdin' on 2 let it go!

Don't know why I'm holdin' on for,
But it's 'bout due time that I know.

I'm thirty years old with nothing to show!
My head hangs low
Full of the "hang lows",
In my head a song plays low,
The volume's low but strong,
Playin' on n' on,
Playin' so long that I hum along;
I Keeeep Hooooldin' Oooooon,
I Keeeep Hooooldin' Oooooon!
The theme song of a hoarder!
I'm a horrible hoarder,
A horrible example for my daughter,
I'm a horrible hoarder
Hoardin' horrible horrors
That have me outta order
N' keep me from being the supporter
That I can be for er'!!
Somethin's wrong;
DO I HAVE A DISORDER??!!!
Cause I hold em', set em' down,
pick em' back up
N' hold em' some more of course!
It's a Tug O' War of sorts
but perhaps lettin' go'll
open the door for,
a new world to explore or
a new life to adore more
but I'm not for sure,
N' I just don't understand
why I keep holdin' on for!

I have a wardrobe of fear n' doubt;
I wear it with me!

It's heavily wearin' in me!
It's all packed up in a time capsule
that's been buried in me!
At times I feel like
a traveling salesman
cause it's like a suitcase that
I carry with me!
At times I'm at odds with God
but I thank em' for barin' with me!
See all I want is happiness n' peace
n' some good peeps ta' share it with me!
But I've held it all.
N' maybe it 8nt all that bad though;
Perhaps I've held it all ta' grow,
N' now I find within my mind
that it's time ta' let it go!

It's time ta' release.
Time ta' release each piece n' re-piece,
Time ta' rise like yeast,
A better *ME* is waitin' to be
unleashed from beneath,
Cause I'm dyin' ta' surface,
My life's been a tragic circus,
I've been like a bad fuse box,
Always ready ta' short circuit!
I'm a run on sentence that
needs ta' be re-worded!
I know I'm far from perfect,
My life is everything I've made it
n' only I can defer it!
Cause Lord knows that
the way things are,

Ain't at all how I'd prefer it!

See I wrote this in advance cause
I knew a change would come to be,
This poem is a message in a bottle
that's self-addressed ta' *ME!!*
I broke it open over a stone
when I withdrew it
from the deep blue sea!
Deep blue sea; drew deep blue *ME.*
Exotic aquatic from the chaotic
of the deep blue "grew" *ME.*
I'm new see, you see a new *ME*
cause I grew free!
I grew free cause I grew tired
of how I used to be!
I grew free from my vices n'
self-destructive devices, cause I said;
"I'm tired of how my life is!"
Tired of feelin' lifeless n' fight-less,
I had ta' fight this
cause I badly wanted ta' right this!
Tired of holdin' my wrongs in a tight grip!
I write this line for my daughter;
My seed n' likeness,
I urge you babygirl
ya' don't wanna be like this!
Or better yet how I was,
but now I'm better because
I knew n' believed n' understood
that my life could
be better than what it was!
In order ta' build

1st ya' have ta' destroy!
I had ta' self-destruct
ta' reconstruct the thoughts in me
n' get back on my feet,
Know what I mean?
I put nightmares ta' sleep,
So I could wake up my dreams!
No longer will I dream
my dreams at nite;
I wanna live em' all in the daylight.
So I had ta' change my life,
Have ta' do what's right,
Although not easy;
Easy doesn't enter into grown up life,
But to get anything of value
1st you have ta' sacrifice!

So it's been a long time coming
n' I have ta' let you know,
That I've learned from *all* I've held
n' now I've learned ta' let it go!

DAD I REMEMBER

I remember the sweet music that pranced
around our living room in the evenings,
And I remember you saving the best tune for last
So that you could ask mom for the last dance.
I remember you callin' mama "Louise"!
I remember you trying to help me
understand the potential I had within.
I remember your words of wisdom that

Many a fatherless child would pay
a king's ransom to possess.
I remember the planes we'd
watch streak above the Lakefront.
I remember Hornets with blue angel wings,
I remember Thunderbirds, F-14's,
F-15's, and FA-117 Stealths!
I loved waiting to hear the sound of afterburners,
a sound worthy of induction into
the Rock N' Roll Hall of Fame nearby!
I remember waking up flat on my back,
Feet raised as if tap dancing on
brake peddles and accelerators,
My hands forming a white-knuckled grip
around an imaginary steering wheel,
After awaking from a long night of dueling it out
against Lil' Al, Mears, Rahal, and Fittipaldi in my dreams!
Unleashing all of our horsepower
beneath the skies on the same grounds.
I remember the fragrance of the West Side Market.
I remember yearning for a Gyro each time we went!
I remember trips to the Cleveland Public Library,
and I remember thinking
that I had never seen so many books in my entire life!
The place seemed like a cathedral
of elephantine proportions to me
because I stood only knee high.
I remember long drives to Toronto and Montreal;
I remember Caribana.
I remember long drives to The Big Apple.
A city that never sleeps or takes
anything even remotely close to a nap.
I remember Sunday walks to Mentor Beach Park;

You, mama, and I.
I remember the rackets we swung,
And the frisbees we would float through the summer's breeze.
The rocks we skipped together that
painted our footprints across Lake Erie.
I remember the three of us sitting on
the swings atop the foliaged hill
overlooking the canvas of Lake Erie.
Us watching the sun take a dip into
the velvet sheet of aqua below,
as if to cool itself off after a long day
of raining it's rays on humanity.
Such a toiling task.

I remember keeping the Sabbath.
I remember saying grace.
I remember pepperpot.
Ginger tea brewed from the roots.
I remember the soothing tones of
Nat King Cole's angelic voice on Christmas mornings.
I remember the quiet.
The calm.
The peace.
Walks to Rini Regos.
I remember my raising.
I remember being with you when you would go
look for spare parts at junkyards.
I remember the day when I was amusing myself
by sitting inside each of the old scrapped vehicles.
Pressing each button and turning every knob
with my tiny fingers until I discovered how to
shift the car from P to R,
and so on and so on.

I remember putting it in neutral and the car began to roll
backwards down the incline!
I remember my heart retreating
downward toward my stomach,
And thanks be to God I remember that
the only thing that saved my ass
was a stack of old tires, somewhat intuitively
positioned at the bottom of the hill!!
I remember the calm demeanor you displayed externally,
I could only imagine what you felt beneath it all.
Funny, the things we remember.

This is just a letter to inform you,
In case you're ever under the impression that I have
suppressed memories,
Or that I may have developed amnesia.
You need not to worry,
My mind is whole and intact,
As are the memories.
And I remember *good* times.
I remember them fondly.
Daddy I remember.
I remember.
I remember.
I remember.
I ....

ACCEPTANCE

God, grant me the serenity to accept the
things I cannot change.
The courage to change the things I can,
and the wisdom to know the difference.
I can't blame nobody for holdin' me back from
being the man that I should be,
The only person holdin' me back now is me.
I must accept who I am and who I have become,
Accept where I am and see how far I've come,
Accept the things I have to do,
Accept the things that I have done,
Accept the fact that I'm a son,
Son of a man,
Son of a man who told me "Son you can."
Who can I trust when I'm in a jam man?
No homies, no comrades, no right-hand man,
I need solid ground on which to stand,
So when it hits the fan,
I put my faith in the Son of Man,
Stop pray and believe,
That if I ask I shall receive,
For whom the Son has set free,
He is free indeed.

Acceptance will lead to discovery.
Acceptance will discover me.
Acceptance will uncover me.
Acceptance, above all other things.

Accept the pain for playin' games,
Accept the certificate of blame I've obtained,

With the signature of my name signed at the bottom,
For all the opportunities I squandered when I got em',
Balls that rolled on my court but I dropped em',
Windows of opportunities closed cause I forgot em',
I have no one else to blame for me hittin' rock bottom,
For my life getting foiled and spoiled and gone rotten,
Accept these facts, accept these things,
Accept the truth and whatever pain it brings,
Accept the consequences and
reverberations of my ill-fated procrastinations,
My lack of pro-activity has lead me to my situation,
Accept the repercussions for doin' nothin',
Gotta start doin' somethin',
I betta start rushin'.
Get busy livin' or get busy dyin'.

When you look at me you may see nothin' special,
Just a walkin' talkin' vessel that wrestles with his flesh,
Well if you look beyond the physical and reach
beyond the visible you will see an individual,
Multi-gifted and three dimensional,
Life is more than just the air that
I breathe or the things that I need,
It's about staying grounded and the things that I believe,
Like raising and teaching my little seed,
So she can be a shining light for the world to see,
She can overcome the world and
be whatever she wants to be,
My seed will be my greatest deed,
and I'll always be there for her in her time of need,
Cause she was assigned to me and I fully accept this.
To this date acceptance is my greatest discovery.
Acceptance has uncovered me.

Acceptance, above all other things.
Acceptance has un-smothered me.
Acceptance has uncovered me.
Through acceptance I've discovered **ME**.

BACK II THE FUTURE...AGAIN

We've ALL seen Back II the Future.
Marty hopping into Doc's Delorean.
Flyin' on hover boards,
scrappin' wit' Biff,
fightin' cowboys,
N' even gettin' hit on by his future mother!
Yeah, Marty McFly.
Fun stuff, cool stuff.
Stuff that made me wanna wake up
to the sight of hover boards floating
under the tree on Christmas morning!

To time travel, to travel time, to travel mine,
n' as I travel I travel in my mind,
Over time I've developed a traveled mind.
But what'll become of what I've left behind?
Words n' actions can travel time.
Don't think so?
Then what about the words n' actions of Christ?
Prophets and philosophers who's words
n' actions originated over 2,000 yrs. ago,
Yet have transcended time,
Leaping thru stargates into other dimensions,
And have resonated in the hearts n' minds
of billions over the course of;

TIME.
Time traveled.
Shakespeare, Frederick Douglas,
Lincoln, Whitman,
n' right down to the views of Langston Hughes,
Kennedy, Martin, Malcolm, Mother Teresa n' Gandhi, Marley,
Vessels that truth spoke thru,
n' who's words n' deeds are only a stones throw away in
the breath of time yet shot off with
a blast that will propel them far beyond
the timelines of generations
That are yet to open their eyes to the light of this world.
TIME.
TIME will travel.
Words n' ideas n' philosophies, n' the deeds
attached to them will travel.
n' they will resonate in the hearts n' minds of
those who are far off.
Words n' philosophies that will have withstood a test.
A test of time.
But the real test is one which is placed WITHIN us,
Rather than BEFORE us.
For everything that travels must reach an ultimate destination.
What will I do when such great words n' ideas,
Philosophies n' deeds reach the destination of me?
When they reach the destination of *you*?
The destination of *us*?
These words are rich, potent, have traveled time yet are
TIMELESS.
Worth all their weight in gold n' fine jewels yet they are
PRICELESS.
How will we utilize them n' implement them not
only into our lives, but the lives of our seeds

N' those who are a far off,
yet to open their eyes to the light of this world?
For the purpose of life is to Live, Love,
Learn, and to leave a Legacy.
A legacy.
Something that will live on for those that follow after our time.
Beyond our time.
Cause time travels.

CHAOS

Good mornin' heartache it's been awhile.
Brushin' my teeth in the mirror hopin' I can brush on a smile!
Wishin' I can brush away misery with a bar of Dial!!
Wipe hurt off my face with a nice warm towel!
Then throw it to the floor to soak my tears up from the tile!
Sometimes I feel this life'll be the death of me!
I try to run n' hide but my conscious just ain't lettin' me!
I'm tryin' ta' leave a legacy but failure keeps upsettin' me!
Time's goin' on n' people are forgettin' me!
Trying to get ahead but the world's gettin' ahead of me!
Lord, help me live up to my pedigree,
Remove the haze so I can see the best in me!
Everyday I feel my destiny so I just can't let it be!
Life's steadily brought me through many changes;
But it's alright; Ledisi.

I think that's my dream in the sky
right where it's s'posed to be,
But doubt is an eclipse that makes it hard
for me to see it's really close to me!
It's like I'm lookin' through tinted lenses n'

The world just ain't as bright anymore!
Ain't really got a crew we ain't tight anymore!
It don't feel like life's worth the fight anymore!
Ain't nothin' right anymore!
Lord why hast thou forsaken me!
Why's it always feel like the world is constantly shakin' me!
Quakin' me! Breakin' me! Blatantly hatin' me!
I'm on a wild goose chase,
n' I just don't know where the hell it's takin' me!
I'm on a Duck, Duck, Goose chase,
but the geese are chasin' *ME!!*
It's makin' me; CRAZY!!!!
At night my dreams keep chasin' me!
Takin' me to a place I can't escape
n' see hell is hot n' it's bakin' me!
Been waitin' up n' waitin' see,
Waitin' n' layin' patiently!
Please hurry up n' awaken me!
From the Wes Cravens I've been havin' lately!
Can't believe how long it's takin', GEEZ!
I'm waitin' PLEASE!
Waitin' just in case to see,
If you got somethin' ta' say to me!
But it just feels like you're playin' wit' me!
How come you ain't savin' me?!!
GOD!!!!

I can't figure out how me n' Destiny went *so* wrong;
n' how I ended up wit'chu!
N' how we grew so strong?!
We don't even get along, we just *go* along!
What the hell's been goin' on?!
How's this been goin' on *so* long?!

We've grown comfortable n' I won't even lie to you,
But Heartache I'm getting' tired of not likin' you!
I think it's best we separate, it's time to say good-bye to you!

ETA (Emajinay's Time for Arrival)

My ol' man threw the gauntlet
Out for me n' I couldn't evade it,
Learn ta' manage your life with honesty
were the words that he stated,
outta disappointment n' love
n' his words were heavily weighted.
Your so jaded n'
there's no mistakin',
Your life's deflated by negativity
n' ya' need ta' negate it.
Some new terms for
your life need to be negotiated,
this is so important
n' it can't be overstated,
ta' give birth to a new beginning
you gotta procreate it!
Don't kick yourself for the
way your life's been made,
just admit that YOU made it!
You're not doin' good now,
but it's up to you ta' go n' change it!
When life's at a stand still,
you can only do what ya' can n' will,
build what ya' can build,
take moments ta' breathe and chill,
cuz' they say sometimes it's best

for ya' ta' just stand still.
But it feels like I got my hands filled,
enough ta' dump in a landfill,
enough to puke out my diaphragm; ILL!!
I wanna get cracked over the head by
Sandman and pass out in a sand mill!
Life's testing my patience, spirit and will,
and I'm standing still in a terminal for hours,
waiting for take off and departure,
I'm in a lay over, I'm way over due to take over,
I can't stay over, everyday's closer
to the day I take flight!
I'm tired of tryin' to get by like the next guy,
on a Red Eye, ready to jet the skies,
trying to make the jet fly!
My stomach's tied in knots as I hit 20 knots,
say a prayer n' wave on the spot
before I take off over the waves n' the rocks.

I ain't boarding a Boeing not knowing where I'm going!
I'm tryin' to go Northwest, Southwest,
to places I've never been to.
Other hemispheres, I'm goin' all Continental!

N' I'm hellbent on gettin' a chance
n' gettin' a break!
I'm testin' fate, it's the chance I'm destined to take,
Tryin' to make the future I'm destined to create.
Using my opticals to see and
overcome all obstacles and mistakes!
It's a lot at stake, and I'll get there one way or another,
So no need ta' wait', guess or estimate,
The time I'll arrive at the gate,

Don't guess-timate; don't wait next to the gate!
Cause I'm already here n' I've already flied, or flew,
or better yet flown; Pan Am.
Endured some turbulence
n' now I'm ready ta' land,
Forget the wagon or joinin' the band!
I gotta vibrate higher!
Tired of bein' n' outkast in this land!
People takin' stuff
right outta my hand!
Time ta' take my power back
n' start pursuin' MY plans!
I am, ready ta' take a stand!
Ta' be better than I've been,
N' be better than I am!
Quick Pavane fast Gavotte
N' a change of stance!
N' a change of prance,
Time to face up to the music n' dance!
Time to wave the old bye-bye!
Adios! Sayonara! From I & I.
No lie, I'ma make the best of my life,
The best of my time,
n' I'ma try n' try till I die,
I'm focused baby n' I'm aimin' sky high,
The harder I try the higher I'll rise,
Gotta strive while I'm alive,
I got one life to live n' I won't stop till I fly!

READY TO RUN

I've ran the streets,
I've ran luck 'till it ran out!
I've ran the wrong way and ran into walls,
I've ran the streets of Madrid;
I've ran with bulls.
I've been trampled.
I've been knocked off the saddle,
Thrown aside and bucked by hooves;
I've been hobbled.

For many years people have told me
I should chase my dreams;
"Run with it!"
"Go with it!"
"Believe n' achieve!"
But I've put it off so long it seems I forgot how to run
n' my muscles have atrophied!
Perhaps procrastination's just a fancy term for "losing steam!"
I'm in a relay of dreams,
Holdin' the baton n' holdin' up the team!
The gun went off years ago n' I'm still at
the startin' line n' way outta the lead!
I feel like I'm way outta my league!
They say that if you ain't afraid of your dreams,
Your dreams ain't big enough;
My dream is huge n' I'm petrified!!
In the words of Shakespeare;
Our doubts are traitors,
and make us lose the good we oft might win,
by fearing to attempt.

I've accomplished failure.
By the wrong application of thought,
the mismanagement of opportunities,
the procrastination of a known purpose.
A power evolving universe has no place for the sluggish.
It's a grind it out world,
N' if you can't walk with the footman,
How you gonna run with the horseman?

On your mark, get ready, set, GO!!
It ain't nothin' to it but to do it; so move it!!
I'm ready to accelerate to a better pace,
I'm ready to chase harder than I've ever chased,
for all that God's intended for me to embrace!
Gotta replace the foulness in my mouth with a better taste!
No time to waste, be clever and make haste,
Don't sit back, let it fester n' wait,
They say 'never say never'
But it's now or never
do it 'now' cause 'never's' too late!
I'm getting' my shoes laced cause I'm ready to race!

I'm ready to run with it now!
The race is not given to the swift
No, but to those that persevere,
Let me run with perseverance,
this race that has been marked out for me.
As I toil under the sun, salt of the Earth.
Toil.
By the sweat of my brow I'll earn my bread.
The Good Book told me that
whatever I put my hands to that I'm to do it
with all of my might.

For the race is not given to the swift, no,
nor the battle to the strong and to all that proceed,
But time and chance happen to them all.
For man does not know his time.
How much time I got?
I got till it's gone!
Cause there is no work or device,
or knowledge or wisdom in the grave.
The place is here, the time is now,
for me to take my place under the sun.
I'll never be what I could've been,
I'll never be "again" who I once was,
So I press forward to what and who I shall become.

THE PACT

I need a new beginning,
A life I can be in accord with,
This is a life I've grown sick n' tired of bein' bored with!
I can't afford this, I need somethin' more,
that I can do somethin' more with!
Without overexertin' n' havin' to force it!
I know it's gotta be somethin' more to this! Life!!
Said it's gotta be somethin' more to this! Right?

I wanna real life,
I wanna fulfilled life, n' I wanna feel life,
n' I want it ta' feel right, real nice!
Livin' free, bein' all that I can be,
all that I can be for me n' my family!
My life ain't for another's hands,
for no other woman or man,

or one's who don't even give a damn!
I got goals n' I got somethin' planned!
I'm sick of livin' life without the itch,
It's time to get up from off my couch
n' get out n' get bout' my ish'!
Ta' get somethin' from out of this gift,
N' I'm goin' off without a hitch!
It's time to get up, get out n' get somethin'
I'll never make it if I never even try!
To be precise n' exact, in fact I'm makin' a Pact!
I'm makin' a Pact, I'm makin' a Pact!
N' I'm reclaimin' my life n' I'm takin' it back!
N' even try n' do n' act better than that!

I vow to the highness I'ma stay in abidance
with the agreement we wrote n' I signed it!
Inscribed with my Bic n' signed with a trident!
Lord I respect n' I fear you,
God, hear ye hear you, help me!
I need somethin' to adhere to, to endear to,
to get me in gear to navigate through this journey
that I'm tryin' to steer through!
Put my past in the rear-view,
and get nearer to the destination that I wanna get near to!
I ain't on Earth for nothin' I'm here to;
Fulfill a purpose n' provide a service,
I got a gift that you gave me n' I don't deserve it,
n' I sure as hell didn't earn it.
God must've seen somethin' stirring beneath the surface
flowin' like a gentle current.
I don't know.
I'm far from bein' perfect
but I must've been worth it!

God bought me time to spend it,
Every cent n' every minute,
for me to use it till' it's finished!
Till' I draw my last breath n' I have nothin' left.
Gotta see everyday as a 2nd chance.
'Cause everyday is like a chance that
could've been gone yesterday!
I stand trial, I stand dialed n' ready a man-child.
I take an oath to solemnly swear,
n' I vow now to somehow get it right **right** now,
Make it all worthwhile, cause I
wanna make the heavens proud!

See I know I made this bed that I'm layin' in,
But I'm ready to change the sheets!
I even think I could use a new Temperpedic
mattress with lumbar support,
N' some new pillows with different cases!
Yeah, a new mattress to evenly distribute comfort to my soul
N' relieve the stress from my pressure points
and prevent bed sores from bruising my purpose.
New pillows to cushion my dreams,
and hold them firmly within' my mind.
I'll lie down fulfilled, and wake up renewed,
with a dream and a purpose in clear focus.
Trust the process-es, stay focused on the object-ive,
Put it all together like an omelet is!
I'm killin' my doubt with the coldest of weapons;
CONFIDENCE!!
To whom much is given much is tested!!!!
I'm bein' tested to make the most with what I'm blessed with!
N' I gotta Man Up n' accept this.
I vow to give my all, to my fullest capacity,

My thoughts and actions are in alliance,
I'm escaping my gravity and defying science!
Out of defiance, I'm out of compliance with the Old Laws,
Got a new direction n' I'm under better guidance,
with a strategy to turn tragedy to triumph!

I vow to be strong Today,
So I can be stronger Tomorrow,
Stronger tomorrow to be stronger for Whatever,
So whatever comes I'll be stronger for Forever.
To be precise n' exact, in fact I'm makin' a Pact!
I'm reclaimin' my life n' I'm takin' it back!

POTENTIAL

All my life I've been told how I have potential.
From my parents, family, friends, teachers,
Acquaintances and complete strangers.
Oh you're so of full potential!
You show great potential!
Potential to give you opportunities
to get into something big too!
You got so much potential; use what God gives you!
The world is your oyster to dig into,
N' you can continue to get into anything on the menu
If you can find a way to fit into the potential God gives you!
N' thru all the things I've lived thru
N' all of the things I've been thru
N' still gotta get thru,
N' no matter how long I sleep on the issue,
That solitary word "potential" always seemed to slip thru,
Like every time the wind blew,

Every time it came around.
But instead of living it up;
I always lived it DOWN.
Let it fall from the sky like leaves to the ground,
Drying up in the sun, turning yellow n' brown!
To be blown n' raked around
N' gathered by the pounds,
Clumped together n' thrown into a compost pile.
See I may have left myself in that pile of compost,
No worries I'll re-emerge as fresh growth!

Dreams I'm holdin;
They are golden.
But they're frozen.
I've been locked away in a tomb,
A bolted room,
An air vacuumed tube,
Years have been stolen,
I've been cryogenically frozen,
With ice sickles clingin' to my toes,
N' a terrified gaze n' my eyes still open,
My hands form an icy grip around the dreams I'm still holdin'!

I'm ready for the thaw.
Ready to emerge with my dreams in my heart
Rather than clinched in my paws.
Ready to press play to get out of pause.
Emerge from the crisp of fall,
Through the tundra n' from under the force
of winter's permafrost jaws,
I'm ready to spring forward with a new cause,
Ready for a new season,

Ready for a new climate,
I can see that mountain n' I'm ready to climb it!
N' though it's impossible to see the entire
mountain while I climb it,
No matter how high it gets,
Or how bright that sky is lit,
Hold on tight can't lose my grip,
If my feet are positioned right I cannot slip,
I won't bust my knees I won't bust my lip,
I'ma keep on pushin' till' I reach the tip!
N' I always did think that the sky looked sweet,
But it'll be even sweeter when I can see it under my feet!
I don't wanna miss it,
spendin' my life lookin' for Golden tickets,
I ain't gotta play the lottery *I AM THE TICKET!!!!*

Understanding potential & potential that is
realized can make me a force!
A force to be reckoned with,
ain't no second guessin' with,
like you don't know who you messin' with
type of force of course.
I'm a reflection of the greatest,
I'm a reflection of that kind of potential
That created the Heavens and the Earth,
who created the beautiful woman that delivered me at birth!
Creator of the Milky Way Galaxy!

If I'm a reflection of that kind of potential
then the Milky Way is the limit!
The word potential minus the i-a-l spells potent.
Something full n' rich that if released
Can alter any n' everything it comes in contact with it!

It can alter dispositions and equilibriums,
It can even alter the course of history!
Her-story, his-story, history exists in me!

So remove Stan the Man n' the Duke of Earl,
Give me a place to stand n' I can move the world!

In the night time I dine,
At a table placed directly underneath a portrait of
The Last Supper.
Could this be mine?
They say the good die young,
so I may not have much time
gotta shine while it's time';
It's my time to shine,
Shine the kinda shine that'll make eyes go blind,
But'll open the blinds of a mind's eye at the same time!
Shine n' grind n' in due time I'll find n' exceed my prime!
Cause I don't just need **A** prime,
I want my whole life to be prime!
Prime n' sublime.
My heart n' my mind filled with subliminal sunshine!
They say the good die young so I may not have time,
to fulfill this God given potential of mine.
So hey potential!
What-up-doe!
I'm callin' to you now!
Can you hear me in there!
I'm ready to pursue,
I'm ready to move,
Ready to face issues I need to unglue n' undo,
I'm ready to be used,

Ready to see a new view,
Ready to see in 3D,
ready to see in new hues,
I'm ready to do anything you need me to do!
Potential I know you've been waiting on me,
But now I'm ready; for you.

CAN I LIVE
(I WANNA LIVE)

From the very start,
I possessed a distinctive characteristic;
DESIRE.
More specifically; the desire to live.
I began engaged in a race for life,
120 million life seeds in the starting blocks at the start line,
Poised to explode at the sound of the gun,
With the force of a tidal wave at my back I was thrust forward,
The chaotic marathon began.
Switching lanes at every turn,
Jostling for position,
Amongst the millions I saw the odds
stacked against me on every side,
But odds didn't matter, for only one thing
and one thing only drove my movement: DESIRE.
I'm gonna cross that line 1st,
I WANNA LIVE!
With the focus of a meditating Buddist,
and John Henry sledgehammer swinging grit, I dug deep,
Swimmin' faster than Michael Phelps himself!
I WANNA LIVE!

In miraculous fashion worthy of ESPN's Top Ten Highlights,
I outlasted my competition,
n' after nine months of incubation
I was born in a flash of white light,
on a late night, to a young woman dancin'
to Soul Train diggin' that disco hype.
I emerged from my triathlon victorious and triumphant,
laid to rest on the belly of the woman I just exited,
Screaming, crying, announcing my arrival to the world,
Screaming; I AM ALIVE!
I WANNA LIVE!
I AM HERE!

My journey began.
The journey of my life.
I began on fire n' full, of desire,
But through the years.
Through the years.
O' through the years.
Something happened.
Something happened to me.
Over the years.
Through the…
Years of people tellin' me I'm not good enough,
For them.
Years of tellin' myself I'm not good enough,
For them.
Years of fallin' short,
Years of thinkin' n' feelin' less than my best,
Like I keep bein' quizzed n' I'm failin' the test,
Years of getting hit by all
the curveballs life threw at me!
Got knots in my soul, I'm cold, n' I'm not happy,

I feel like a piece of crap that's been
ran over n' backed over twice!
I'm so crappy!
What the hell happened!
24/7's have piled up on each other n' I feel like I'm slackin',
I feel like I can't go on n' somethin' is lackin',
What the hell happened!
Somethin' must, have happened,
What the hell happened!
Somethin' must, have happened,
Something happened to that thing…
That…
That thing…
That, thing called DESIRE.
My desire needs fixin',
My desire needs fixin' my desire stopped tickin'.
I feel like a clock.
So much like a broken clock.
Both of my hands have stopped,
I feel like a broken clock.
I'm at a standstill, both of my hands have stopped,
No more tick-tick,
No more tock-tock,
My hands have stopped,
I feel like a broken clock.

'Cause daily life can be so redundant,
Especially on days at the job when my eyes
are fixated on that clock,
I'll find myself thinking that that clock must be arrogant,
Cause it's always stuck on itself,
Even when it feels like time's movin' fast it's like;
"How long's this day gonna last?" I ask.

But eventually the time'll pass at last, n' I gasp.

Feelin' stuck; like the clock on that wall is.
I wanna be free.
For I am not a clock, or just some obscure
piece of décor hung up on some wall,
No, I am more.
I AM LIFE.
George Bernard Shaw was quoted saying that;
"Youth is wasted on the young."
Lord I can't be the epitome of that quote,
Lord I can't allow myself to be like the clock on that wall,
Lord I can't me be like the clock on that wall;
I **promise** I won't be like the clock on that wall!
I will allow myself to be carried away
by the winds of life, not be stuck like a leaf
on the roof of a car,
but to allow the winds to peel me from that roof,
thrown into the jet-stream strapped to a
hang glider riding the current,
navigating over the landscapes of life,
for however long the gusts persist.
I WANNA LIVE!
Lord don't allow me to be like that clock;
I am not a clock.
DESIRE;
Rekindle my desire.
Desire is what got me here,
Let desire be what keeps me here.
Firmly planted in my journey,
Keeping me steadfast,

Living totally in the present,
Fully present in the occasion,
Because *LIFE IS AN OCCASION*;
And *I WANNA RISE TO IT.*
CAN I LIVE?
I WANNA LIVE;
for the Eve who insisted that I should keep running,
for the woman who told me;
Prove em' wrong son,
can't nobody think anything negative about you
if you don't give em' good reason to,
Prove em' wrong son.
For the one good childhood friend who always told me;
I don't wanna hear anything else about your art n' poetry,
Until you do something with em',
All I hear is talk, you make me sick man,
I would kill to have what you have,
I wanna live for my daughter who needs
that positive role model in her life,
For the youth that needs one as well,
And for this young man who needs to
come to the realization that
he is one of God's greatest creations.
That he is so much more than a clock hung up on some wall,
or just some obscure piece of décor;
No, I am more.
I AM LIFE.
I WANNA LIVE!
CAN I LIVE?
I wanna live, I wanna give,
I wanna live, live, live,
N' I wanna give, give, give,
I wanna give all the love that a heart can give,

N' soak in all the love that a heart can soak in,
n' I wanna give; It back.
I wanna give my all so that when it's my time,
I can truly feel I've left nothin' behind,
No worries, no cries,
No sad good-bye's,
I can leave the world with today in my eyes.
No one can say "He didn't try."
Cause I did.
N' I can leave the world proud of the way;
THAT I LIVED.

PART 2
1st OFFENSE
INCOGEGO

IncogEGO

THE BLOGS AND JOURNALS
OF AN INTROVERTED SOUL

"Some people put the best outside,
some people keep the best inside."
-BOB MARLEY

ODDBALL

I was a people lover and free spirited. I used to always love being in groups, laughing, connecting, and I was always the class clown in school. I grew up very sheltered. Dad didn't let me out much. I was a bit of a cut up in school, so he grounded me often, I mean like, for *entire* summers. He was extremely strict, and I was extremely rambunctious. I wouldn't say I was bad, well not in elementary school at least, I just wanted to be a kid, not a robot. As I said, I was very sheltered, I barely watched TV, no video games, no friends came over, I wasn't allowed to go to any of my friends houses to play or sleep over, and life at home was quiet. So I viewed school as my time to be free, to be a kid, to have fun with my peers. By the time I got to junior high I had come to terms with the fact that this is my life, I'll never be able to be myself any other way, or at any other time. So I cut loose and let it all hang out. When I was at Shore Jr. High, man I was hell on wheels, aka. I'm quite positive that in my 7th and 8th grade years I set the record for the most detentions and suspensions ever given to any kid who had gone there for three whole years. As a result I was kicked out before the 9th grade year even began. If I don't hold the record, than I'm definitely in the Top 5. Shore had never seen the likes of me before, and they may never see the likes of me again. I was truly one of a kind.

After 8th grade, I spent a year in a program for bad ass kids (they might as well had named it just that), it was called The SBH Program, for *Severally Behaviorally Handicapped* students. Essentially, it was the alternative to DH (the detention home). I was shipped off to Memorial Jr. High, on a short bus with kids who were doped up on Ritalin and God knows what else. I myself didn't need that crap like the other kids. Some of the kids who were in SBH with me, you could tell that they really had a problem, a true handicap. You wanna know what landed me in that place, or rather the reason I was acting out in first place? I was acting out for the attention I felt I wasn't receiving at home. Not to mention the fact that I was bottled up 24/7, I couldn't go anywhere or do anything, I had no outlets, so when I went to school, the cork popped off!! Anyway, 9th grade was my first trouble free year of school, well, not totally trouble free, I kicked a kid's butt in the library once, and got suspended for it. But other than that, I was good. From there I got out of SBH and went on to Mentor High School to start 10th grade.

I was a chameleon of sorts in my school days, in the sense that I could go in and out of any clique there was. I would sit at the lunch table with the geeks one day, then slide down and hang with the *cool* kids the next. I got along with everybody. High school now, was a whole other type of monster. A new hierarchy was in order now. Over 3,000 kids in one place, all trying to find their way, and their place in this new society. The world had just tripled in size. It was challenging; cliques were bigger, girls were prettier, and the whole nine yards. Not to mention I was one of maybe a dozen black students in the entire school. Back then I remember I could count every one of us, not including myself, with my two hands. Dating was a big thing in HS too, for me, it was rather my *lack* of dating. Lol. I had never been much of a ladies guy in school, and the fact that I was so sheltered didn't help. The only girlfriend I had was in the 4th grade, her name was Pamela and she dumped me after 3 days because I couldn't come outside or talk to her on the phone. Years earlier I had been scarred by an incident in the 1st first grade at Lake Elementary that also didn't help my cause. I had a crush on a girl named Colleen, a gorgeous girl with curly black hair and golden bronze skin. I made the 1st grader mistake of telling one of the other kids that I liked her, and the kid wasn't supposed to say anything, *it was a secret*. But you already know how that turned out, don't you? She found out, everyone was talking about it, and I was embarrassed. Anyway, while we were sitting around, she told me that the two of us couldn't be boyfriend and girlfriend. I was shocked, and I asked her why, and she said that we couldn't be boyfriend and girlfriend because; *'you're black, and I'm white.'* I was blown away, hurt, and even confused, because remember when I described her just little bit ago, I said that she had *curly black hair and golden-bronze skin*, right? So I was like, *"What do you mean, you're black too!"* Then she informed me that she was mixed; her mom was Hawaiian and her dad was white. BOOM! Although I went on to have some *puppy-drying-humping-love* with a few white girls in the years that proceeded this, that moment really messed my world up a bit. My subconscious was stained by the memory straight up to high school and into adulthood. In the back of my mind, if a girl didn't like me or wasn't interested, *I knew why*.

My priorities in HS were, uh, outta whack. Class work, didn't matter. Homework, didn't matter. Dang, I barely passed gym and I even got a D in *art class*. Oooooh, I know right, the artist that failed at his own game. Yeah, that's pretty messed up. Academically, I was *tore up* from *the floor up*, it even cost me my place on the football team. But I hey, I wanted to party on Friday nights, hang out during the school week, and I blew off my homework assignments in the process. My GPA was abysmal. But I was caught up in the hierarchy of high school life, and nothing else mattered to me. I was having fun, sadly, at my own expense. Hell, I loved school so much, I even went to summer school in both my sophomore and junior years. *Blah.*

In my senior, Mom left pops (for a moment) and we moved to Painesville, OH. I enrolled at Fairport Harbor High School, it was a small school in a small town, a far cry from Mentor High. I stepped in that place an was like, *WTF!* Man I bounced outta that place like I stole somethin', *lol!* The only good thing I got outta that school was the girl that I lost my virginity to, *lol!* Alright, alright, let me get serious again. < *in my serious voice* > After about a month or two at Fairport I split and went to Harvey High School. Much better. Harvey was a melting pot, a diverse mix of ethnicities. Painesville in general is a melting pot, populated by blacks, whites, hispanics, etc. I loved it. But I was sort of an oddball in this mix. My whole life prior to being there I was the *only* black kid in all of my classes. All of my friends and classmates were white. I grew up listening to rap, rock, and alternative. My white buddies and I dyed our hair and had piercings. They knew me as the *whitest* black kid they knew, and in all truthfulness, for a lot them, I was the **only** black kid they knew. So when I got to Harvey, I was *The Black White Kid*, aka the *Dalmatian*, aka the *Alien*, aka *ET the Black Extraterrestrial*. I was awkward, but I was still the chameleon. Still floating from clique to clique, still slacking and blowing off homework, smoking cigarettes in the bathroom, leaving during lunch hours with a couple of kids and returning in time for study hall, blowed out of my mind, reeking with the scent of cannabis. I fit perfectly into the category assigned for the *lost ones.* I was a ball of confusion. My purpose for life was unclear, I mean, I knew I could write and draw, but that just wasn't where my focus was. I was looking for fulfillment, love, acceptance, and ultimately myself, in all the wrong places. Before the end of my senior year, I was called into the counselors office to discuss my academics. My grades were so bad that the counselor actually recommended to me that I should intentionally drop out of school because there was absolutely no way I would've been able to graduate with the rest of the class. He suggested that I drop out, forfeit the remainder of the school year, take summer courses and return in the fall to pick up the remaining credits needed for me to graduate. I didn't do either one. I dropped out....in the 12th grade. That was it, 18, a drop out, lost, with no future, and I felt like a monumental failure. I earned my GED a year or so later but it was a small consolation. I had no plans for anything, I was an aimless drifter. At that time I began to withdraw from the world. I grew depressed, confused, suicidal, lonely, and bitter towards my father, and even towards my mother. For after all, it takes two to raise a child, thus, in my eyes, she became an accomplice. I blamed everybody else and *everything* else for all my problems. *Woe Is Me.* I was clinging to the past, scared of the future, and lost in the present. I began to feel like I couldn't relate to anyone anymore. I became an alien in my own skin. I faded out, and withdrew into the shadows. I became *invisible.*

THE UNCOMFORTABLE COMFORT ZONE

"You won't find the solution by saying there is no problem."

Living with a Perceived Case of Agoraphobia

The black hole of depression pulled me in, tore me apart, molecule by molecule, reconstructed my entire DNA sequence save for a few genomes, and deposited me somewhere outside of the known universe in which we live as a man I barely recognized. I seriously did not know who I was anymore. I mean of course I knew my own name, date of birth, my gender, where I was born, etc. But it was as if while exiting the Stargate into that unknown dimension, when the cosmic forces reconstructed me it left something out and inserted something else in it's place. I was fully cognitive, aware, conscious, and present in this new place, this new dimension, but my powers had stayed behind to float freely in the universe of my origin. Till this day, I've been trying to find that missing component.

The dimension that I'm speaking of, is the comfort zone, or rather, the Uncomfortable Comfort Zone, the UCZ. I've locked myself away in this thing, this UCZ. It's a Catch 22 because I call myself playing it safe, coping, making myself comfortable through avoidance, but at the same time I was actually making myself *more* uncomfortable.

The mind tricks that Anxiety/Depression/Agoraphobia play can create powerful illusions in the mind. I was tricked into believing that this was my new normal, or, maybe I was born this way, and there is nothing I can do about. I can never escape the UCZ, actually, it has made me second guess the very desire to escape. For why should I want to escape this place, I'm comfortable here, right? NO. There is *no* comfort to be found in a comfort zone. To be in a comfort zone can be likened to being in a prison for your heart, mind, and soul. Better yet, it can be likened to laying in a ditch, weighed down by 50 tons of granite. The comfort zone only creates the *illusion* of comfort. In my experience in the so-called comfort zone, I'd become sluggish, lethargic, very passive, unengaged, reclusive, and living with zero passion. As I mentioned in the opening, I entered into this UCZ universe with something missing, well, there it is. My passion, gone. My energy, gone. My thirst, hunger, and love for life, gone. Many times I'd ask myself, *Where did it go? When did it die?* The truth is, it died the moment I got *comfortable* in there. Without passion, *everything* dies. Dreams die. Enthusiasm dies. Hope dies. Friendships die. Relationships die. Lastly, and worst of all, people die. I had been lulled to sleep, living under the illusion of comfort, while my life had laid itself down in a ditch of despair. Now what?

The diagnosis had been issued. The admission had been made. That's the easy part right? The tough part, and the next question is; *"Ok, what do I do about it?"* My good friend Des once told me, *"If there's anything that's preventing you from being YOU, then you have to find whatever that thing is and get it out of there!"* I'll add to this by saying, I must also place back that which has been removed, lost, misplaced, stolen, or forgotten.

"The man who does not shrink from self-crucifixion can never fail to accomplish the object upon which his heart is set." *James Allen, author of As A Man Thinketh*

My heart is set on being *FREE.* Eric Thomas, aka ET The Hip Hop Preacher, a motivational speaker who is right out of The D and one of my favorite sources of inspiration, says that one of the most important things to do to accomplish anything in life is to become the *Right Person.* In other words, I like to say, *"You can't BE Yourself, if you can't SEE Yourself."* In seeing, what I mean is to understand that this life that I've been living has been an illusion. This comfort zone, agoraphobia, although it all feels so real, it's all in illusion. It's a false representation of who and what I really am. This is not me. This is not normal. I was not born to be this way.

The Good Book has this to say about it; *"…God has not given us the spirit of fear; but of power, and of love, and of sound mind." 2 Timothy 1:7*

Power. Love. Sound mind. PASSION. In my journey to rediscovery, and to regaining my life, these are the components I seek to reattain. These are the components that I must regain possession of, and introduce back into the composition of my souls DNA sequence. To get my very life back into sequence. As I reemerge from the black hole.

LONELIEST MAN ALIVE:
Agoraphobic vs. Being Introverted

"I hate my life, what I've become."

"I suffer from Agoraphobia/Social Anxiety/Depression."

"I have no friends, no life, don't go much of anywhere."

"It's something that's choking the life out of me day by day, minute by minute. It's coiled itself around me like a boa constrictor, suffocating me."

"I wear a facade. I masquerade with a smile, I've always been humorous, but I've trained myself to use my humor as my mask, to hide my pain and hurt."

"I'm able to go to work for 8 plus hours and pull it off. I have everyone thinking I'm this happy go lucky guy who never gets down. I'm cool, I'm funny, and outgoing. But in reality, when the show is over, and the curtain closes, I'm all alone behind that curtain. Shut in. Miserable. Lonely. Sad."

"Alive but not living, I lie the same lie everyday: I'm alright, ain't nothing wrong, I'm just fine." As Lil' Wayne put it in one his songs, "Just to keep from crying, I laugh." It's even hard for me to smile at times, but I choose to. I've been living with this for years. I'm able to work and act and feel normal only at certain places or with certain people that I'm comfortable with. But mainly I masquerade and try my best to cover up how I feel and what I feel, which is just lonely. I don't have friends, no social life. I go to work and come and close the door to the world behind me."

These were my thoughts when I was a "self-diagnosed" Agoraphobic. Agoraphobia vs. Introversion, this had been my dilemma for a long time, until I got clear on the terminology:

Agoraphobia, according to the Medical Dictionary's definition, is the abnormal fear of being helpless in a situation from which escape may be difficult or embarrassing and is characterized often by panic or anticipatory anxiety and finally by avoidance of open or public places.

People with agoraphobia don't feel safe anywhere in the general public, especially in large crowds. Some may only feel safe in their home, and may never step a foot outside.

On the other hand;

"Introversion is an inward orientation to life, and extroversion is an outward orientation. Though you probably use both introversion and extroversion, one of these orientations usually feels more like home – more comfortable, more interesting and more energizing – than the other. Introverts prefer introversion; we tend to gain energy by reflecting and expend energy when interacting. Extroverts have the opposite preference; they tend to gain energy by interacting and expend energy while reflecting."

- Laurie Helgoe, PhD, Introvert Power

To sum it all up; Agoraphobia is choosing to be alone out of fear, and being introverted is choosing to be alone because it is a natural state of being. I'm not afraid of people at all, it's just that "extroverted" socializing drains my battery rather quickly. I enjoy my time to myself to recharge, or better yet, to *stay* charged. As both a person and an artist I am learning that I must embrace being alone. I must turn the tables on *loneliness* and reverse the *order of power* to point towards myself, rather than to forfeit my power to *loneliness*. I had been duped by the Ego, tricked into seeing my solidarity as a weakness, when it is in all truthfulness, my strength. I must embrace it. Very much in the same way Albert Einstein did. Einstein would sit alone, for hours and hours and hours and hours upon *more* hours in silence, contemplating the universe and all of it's wonders and infinite possibilities. Had he not devoted himself to his solidarity, but instead chose to view it as his weakness and lessen himself in the process, than surely he would not have grown into his greatness and be remembered as perhaps the greatest physicist of all time.

For those of us who suffer with any form of anxiety, we are not alone. Perhaps we are alone in the physical sense, but not in the spiritual. Whatever your faith is, there is a divine presence that is on your side. Yes, we may be alone, but in that space, is where we can tap into a great power and source of strength, and find the answers to the questions that riddle us.

"You may be the cause of your problems, but you are also the solution." -unknown

We must listen to the true voice within', trust that voice, and it will never steer us wrong.

PILGRIMAGE INTO EXTROVERSION

When I first retreated into solitude I diagnosed myself as an Agoraphobic with social anxiety and depression. I was freaking out. I didn't know why I felt so overwhelmed. I was over analyzing everything about myself and my life. *What was wrong with me? Why aren't I like everybody else?* etc. I was angry at myself, I internalized many negative thoughts and feelings towards myself, e.g- *I'm weak, I'm lame, I'm boring, worthless*, etc. I made myself feel guilty for not fitting in and being like everyone else. But as time passed I found that I wasn't deathly afraid of being in public, I was just more comfortable being in my own company. Thus, I no longer fit the agoraphobia diagnosis. It was a huge burden to have lifted off of my conscious.

Laurie Helgoe wrote something that she learned from Stephen Rechtshaffen (founder of the Omega Institute), she mentions that Rechtshaffen *observed that it is common for people to become depressed at first when they begin to retreat,* and that *once they settle into solitude, they remember why they came and they find what they came for and more.*

I experienced social anxiety because I was forcing myself to be socially extroverted when I really preferred to be introverted and to have my own space. Not because there was necessarily something wrong with me. I was just putting myself in too many situations that overstimulated me. Some anxieties simply manifest when we try to be something or someone we're not, or when we involve ourselves with people we shouldn't be involved with, and when we place ourselves in surroundings that make us uncomfortable. To sum it all up, I created my own anxiety and agoraphobia, that ultimately lead to my depression. I was sick of being *the kid in the house,* I wanted to take the show on the road, and to be *out there.* I thrusted myself into the extroverted world, and before long I had become overstimulated, out of balance, and out of touch with myself. In which case, I had to withdraw, not out of panic, but out of necessity, it was my nature, it was the healthy thing to do, and I was willing and ready for it. Recharge. Lesson learned: Stay true to your true nature and you will alleviate a lot of unwanted anxieties.

Another fruitful lesson I learned was not to blame anyone else or anything else for my anxiety. Look, if a certain place makes you anxious, then stop going there. If a certain person makes you anxious, then stop messing around with that person! If not completely, then limit your interaction with them as much as possible.

We must realize and understand that we often offer up an open invitation to the stresses we experience. We literally R.S.V.P stress and anxiety. We reserve a table for it, we make room on the guest list for it, we make a parking spot available for it, leave our doors unlocked and wide open for it, etc. For example, I hear people complain all the time about how this person talks behind my back! Well why is that? *You* are the one that told *them this that and the other,* so don't put the blame on them because *You* gave them that power. Their backstabbing started the moment *you* told them *this-that-and the other.* Don't think or say; This person gives me anxiety. NO. If you stop and think long and hard enough you will realize the truth, 'I gave them the key to open the door to anxiety.' The solution is very simple; Watch *what* you say, and **who** you say it to.

Think of it like this, if you were to have a conversation with the person who is supposedly causing you to have anxiety and express your feelings to them, and the word anxiety is mentioned, would you tell them? A) This is *my* anxiety. or B) This is *your* anxiety. Do you follow me? Do you feel me? To say that the anxiety is *theirs* would be the same as having a migraine and telling the other person that it's *their* migraine! The other person may appear to you to be the cause of your anxiety, but this is not true, if you continue to involve yourself with this person (place or thing), then *you* are the cause. Yes the interaction is 50/50, but you have the right to withdraw your portion of that 50 at anytime. See, just the thought alone of dealing with this other person makes anxiety a pre-existing condition, involving yourself with them only increases it. Like the migraine, you may wake up with it, making it a pre-existing condition, but when you expose yourself to some bright lights or noise it only increases it. In this case the next logical thing to do is to avoid that lighting and noise as best as you can. Nonetheless it's your migraine, nonetheless it's your anxiety and you're ultimately responsible for it. It's *yours* and only *you* can alter it. We are the cause of our problems, and we are also the solution to our problems. In his book *As A Man Thinketh*, James Allen explains this in various passages throughout the book;

Man is buffeted by circumstances so long as he believes himself to be the creature of outside conditions, but when he realizes that he is a creative power, and that he may command the hidden soil and seeds of his being out of which circumstances grow, he then becomes the rightful master of himself.

Circumstance does not make the man; it reveals him to himself.

….man is the causer of his circumstances….

A man's weaknesses and strength, purity and impurity, are his own, and not another man's; they are brought about by himself, and not by another; and they can only be altered by himself, never by another. His condition is his own, and not another man's. His suffering and his happiness are evolved from within. As he thinks, so he is; as he continues to think, so he remains.

The answer lies in the way we think. By changing the way we think we can change the way we respond. Change the way we respond, then we can change the outcome of any situation.

We all are familiar with the old cliches; *If I knew then what I know now*, and *hindsight is 20/20*, well, in *hindsight if I knew then what I know now*, the aftershocks would not have reverberated so far into my future. I can just imagine how many nights I could have spared myself from contemplating over *what I was missing out on*. Thoughts such as; *It's a Friday night, I just got paid, and so many other people are out on the town sowing their wild oats and living it up. Yet here I am all alone, watching TV or writing a poem about my hapless existence.* All of that could have been avoided sooner had I realized this truth. Anyway, another cliche says, it's better late than never.

THE NOT SO SUPER......MAN

Dealing with Agoraphobia, Social Anxiety, and Depression has always been something difficult to talk about, especially as a man. No doubt, it is a difficult issue for any human being, regardless of gender, but I want to address this thing from a man's point of view. We men, have the dubious reputation for not being great communicators. This is problematic in our relationships with our significant others, our children, our family, and friends. Also, when dealing with emotional issues such as depression, anxiety, etc. The expectation placed on a man throughout the entire existence of mankind is to be like a superhero. The Man of Steel. Stronger than a locomotive, faster than a speeding bullet, *blah-blah-blah*. But the truth is, and this may come as a shocker to many, *we are human!* We hurt, we suffer, and we struggle with mental illness just like anybody else. We bleed. Depression. Bi-polarism. Social Anxiety. Detachment Disorders. We experience them all.

Some are extroverted, while others are introverted, but never *crazy*.

"The worst thing to call somebody is crazy. It's dismissive...I don't understand this person, so they're crazy....that's bull***. These people are not crazy. They're strong people...."

-Dave Chappelle

Dismissing someone because they have a problem is in itself problematic. A person may have a certain problem(s), but it doesn't make them insignificant, it makes them *human*. When a person is labeled as crazy, it dismisses their *humanity*, even *our* humanity as a whole, and it happens far too often. There's already the unfortunate stigma attached to mental illness as it is, why go and call someone crazy on top of it? Anyway, let me get to the topic; *the fellas*. I feel it's harder on us to communicate our issues and this is why. As men we are taught to be tough, strong, resilient, never to cry, or show any weakness or emotional vulnerability. We are invincible, indestructible; Superman. We are raised being told to; WALK THAT CRAP OFF!! STICK YOUR CHEST OUT!! BE A *MAN*!! So what makes it so hard for a man to open up and get shit off his chest? Geez, I wonder.

Let me paint a big picture of the stigma of mental illness as it pertains to the male species, and what it does to men not only in our society, but around the world. If you're a fan of the NFL, then you remember the name Junior Seau. Seau was an All-Pro, Hall of Famer, a defensive master who struck fear into the heart of every quarterback and ball carrier who ever lined up on the other side of the ball from him. Off the field he was a teddy bear, a man who was giving of himself, his time, and his resources. He was good to his family, his friends, his teammates, he was a philanthropist, the whole nine yards. But at the end of the day he was a man that was 6 foot 3, and weighed 250 pounds. He was a giant of a man, a warrior, a linebacker, #55, with a *manly* image to uphold. But he had demons, and he suffered from a deep depression which caused him to make several unsuccessful attempts at suicide before the final attempt claimed his life for good. Gone at the young age of 43. When anyone takes their own life, regardless of who they are, many are left asking, *why?* In Junior's case, it was no different. *Why? Why would he do this?* Especially when he appeared to have the world on a string. He was a professional athlete making millions, with thousands of admires. Well, as they say, appearances can be deceiving. Here we arrive at the stigma: How can this giant of a man tell someone that he's suffering from depression? How can he look to another man, who's only 5' 9", or a woman who's only 4' 11", and admit his weakness? Because after all, *hey man, aren't you a Pro Bowler, a Hall of Famer? Don't you demolish other men who are just as big as you, if not even bigger for a living? You mean to tell me that you can handle all of that, but you can't handle depression?* Remember, like I said, we men are not trained to be whiners. It's just not MACHO. So what was Junior to do?

*WALK THAT CRAP OFF! QUIT CRYING ABOUT IT! STICK YOUR CHEST OUT! BE.... A ....**MAN**!!!!*

We men are engraved with the *weight room mentality* of; *"DON'T BE A F'n P***Y!!"* The soldiers mentality; *Rub some dirt into your bullet wounds and keep on fighting!* But where do you go, what do you do, when the facade begins to fail you? When it's hard for you to keep telling the jokes and wearing the smile any longer? When it's hard to just be, *macho*? Where can you run and hide? Who can you call? Some like myself, who also had contemplated suicide years ago, but chose seclusion. Isolation. Others reach for the bottle. Many others tie on the tourniquet, thump the vein and reach for the syringe. Some try to smoke it away, snort it away, or pill pop it away. All in a desperate attempt to rediscover their true self and make the demons disappear. But in the end they're left empty, like the bottle, the syringe, and the bowl. Lastly, and unfortunately, many follow the path that Junior chose for himself. The Point of No Return. The Ultimate Sin; taking away the very breathe that The Creator blew into our bodies.

In the aftermath of his death, one of Junior's family members was later quoted saying, *"If he had only talked to me…."* My friends, communication, or actually the lack thereof, is a *huge* problem, amongst men specifically. Until we learn to communicate more efficiently as men (and as all people), undiagnosed illnesses and suicides will continue to occur. It's not about being Clark Kent, who can instantly spin in a phone booth and emerge as the all-powerful Superman, it's about **staying alive**. Yes, it's hard to be a man in this world today, when for so long our image has being in direct relation to The Man of Steel, The Caped Crusader, The Dark Knight. The Hero; who through all adversity never cries, never whines or complains, but accepts his fate and fights through the forces of evil at all costs. But this is not the silver screen, and we are not trying to make a hit at the box office fellas. Yes, fight to the end by all means, but when it's our very lives that are at stake, this is too hefty a cost for one to leave dangling in the balance. If you're hurting in your heart, it's not about being macho. It's about opening that heart, along with the lines of communication. We need to end the silence, and end the Stigma.

INVISIBLE: THE SILENT GIFT

"Your need for acceptance can make you invisible in this world."

-Jim Carrey

The need for acceptance and wanting to fit in, as I explained in the Oddball blog, made me *invisible*, not only to the world but to my very self. Because when you're looking *without*, it's impossible to be able to see *within*. I remember explaining my feeling of invisibility to my Aunt Jackie once. It was late in the summer of 2013, I was over a year removed from a horrible relationship with an ex-girlfriend, and I had been homeless a few months prior to our conversation. It was a struggle to keep my head above water financially, and I was lonely and wishing I could find a good woman to love and that would love me. Along with this I was struggling with *the dream,* and fearing it would never come to pass.

First, let me ask this; Have you ever had that feeling where you wished certain people or that certain someone could know who you really are? Like that, *'if only they knew'* type of feeling? *If only they knew what type of person I really am. If only that girl or that guy knew how well I could love them and treat them right. If only they knew how caring I am....how much fun I can be....how talented I really am....etc.* If you know this feeling, than you can understand what I'm about to talk about. This is a feeling I grew oh so familiar with. I explained this to Aunt Jackie in a telephone conversation that summer. I explained to her that I felt like I'm walking around on this earth carrying a gift, and I have things inside of me that no one knows about, or even cares about. I'm single, I'm lonely and I can't get a date to save my stinkin' life! After sharing this with her, in her sweet Guyanese accent, she gave her reply, and this is some of what she said;

"Brian, others may not know, may not recognize, and may not notice you, but God does. God notices, God knows. God knows You, and He knows what He placed deep inside of you. Never think of yourself as invisible, because you're not invisible to Him...there are so many people in this world who have something that only God and themselves know about....some can paint, some can write, but only God knows. They call it a silent gift...Brian, that's what you are. You are a silent gift. You always have been. To me, you are my Van Gogh, my Rembrandt, Picasso, Michelangelo, all in one. And you are not alone, God knows what you have, and when the time is right, that thing that He placed inside of you is gonna come out to the world."

What a powerful affirmation. I love my Aunt Jackie so dearly, words cannot explain. Her kind words of encourage-ment and her love have meant the **universe** to me. I have learned to take the focus off of the world, and place it on my life, my responsibilities as a man, a father, and the responsibility of being the artist I was created to be. Nothing else matters. I mean, check it out, how was I expecting to fit in when I was in places that I wasn't really meant to fit in the first place?!! I mean, all that year and a portion of the previous year, I had been spending time in a bar populated with blue collar folks. People who sat around discussing plumbing, construction, discussing their day at the office, their day in the court room, etc. Where does a poet, illustrator, and an airbrush artist fit in? I'm from an entirely different dimension. Frankly, though it's been a process for me, I'm finally to the point where I don't care anymore, I'm too old to give a damn. Look honey, I'm an artist, I'm introverted, even a little odd at times, all my life I've been, *from the cradle to the grave.* Deal with it.

This brings me to the next phase of this blog; *KEEP PUSHING, NO MATTER HOW HARD IT GETS AND NO MATTER HOW MUCH RESISTANCE YOU HAVE TO DEAL WITH.* In life, when we're pursuing our dreams or our life's calling, no matter who we are or what it is we're pursuing, we will deal with resistance. Read The War of Art by Steven Pressfield to fully understand the term resistance in the context that I'm about to explain it. Resistance, is the thoughts we hear in our minds that tell us *we are not good enough, not smart enough, we can't do it, it's too hard, we aren't worthy, etc.* That alone is enough to deal with, but I wanna talk about the Resistance that comes from the outside; other people. We have all had others tell us what we can't do, and what we shouldn't do. They've told us *it's impossible, it's too hard, it's stupid, ridiculous, it'll never work, and you will never succeed.* The negative vibe that stems from this is a force to be reckoned with, and it can paralyze our dreams and aspirations if we are not careful. These words can come from anyone, but the cut that goes the deepest is when we hear these things from the ones we love.

Allow me to tell you a story, if you would, about an ex-girlfriend of mine. We met when I moved to Michigan from Ohio in 2001. I was deeply in love with her, she was drop dead gorgeous, I wanted her from the moment I laid my eyes on her. She knew I was into writing poetry, she knew I had a skill for it, she should have, after all, I wrote her poetry all the time. But even though she knew my skill, and that I had a love for writing, she didn't believe in my dream. She was a fundamentalist. She lives with the belief that we all should just do what we know is going to put food on the table. In her words, *"you should only do the **for sure thing**."* She would tell me, *'it's good that you wanna write poetry and all, but you just can't make it in that line of work.'* This is what she believed in her heart, and it *crushed* me. To further explain how deeply she believed in this, let me describe a scenario that took place. In 2003, Musiq Soulchild was one of the hottest R&B acts on the music scene, and he was one of my favorite artists at the time. I had been writing for a bit, both poetry and songs. I had heard on the radio that he was going to be at a club in downtown Detroit one particular evening, and I was hellbent on getting downtown to get an opportunity to meet him and possibly let him get a look at my songs. I called the radio station several times throughout the day to get the number of the venue he'd be performing at that night. After countless attempts I finally got through to the station, I got the number to the club, then all I had to do was find a way to get in. I had no money, but that didn't matter, I had no interest in partying and drinking or anything else, I just wanted an opportunity to meet *the man*. I called the club over and over until I got through, when I did I asked to speak to the owner himself. I earnestly explained to him that I was a poet and a songwriter, and that I wanted to come to the event only to get a chance to meet Musiq and let him take a look at my work. The owner was hesitant at first, but by the end of the conversation I had convinced him to grant my entrance into the club *free of charge!* As you can suspect, I was ecstatic! I couldn't wait to get there, and most of all, I couldn't wait to tell my girlfriend what I was about to do. She came home from work that evening and I told her about what was going down. To my dismay, she was ho hum about it. *"Yeah that's good, but how are you going to get there? I don't want you to use my car to go down there."* Oh yeah, I didn't have my own car at the time and I relied on her as my mode of transportation, and she was never willing to let anyone else driver *her* car, even me, her boyfriend. I had no friends that I could get a ride from, only her, my companion, my lover, my soulmate. I was trusting that she would share my enthusiasm, and be on board and help me pursue my dream. But no, she shot me down. I know right, you're probably thinking, *are you serious?* Yes my friends, I know. I couldn't believe it myself. It's like, I just told you that I could possibly have a meeting with someone who could change my life forever, and not just my life, but our lives, you, me, and our child, and you won't help me try to make this happen? But she did not budge. All of the time I spent on the phone with the radio station, and talking to the owner of the club just went to hell! It was all for nothing. Well, I won't say that it was all for nothing, because that night I learned something very valuable about her, and about relationships in general. If you're going to be with someone, it is of the ultimate importance that you are with someone who believes in you. Someone who will support you, your dreams, and be by your side through the thick and thin. She did not support me, and it crushed my whole world. Ultimately, our relationship did not last, the sensitive poet was not good enough for this particular princess. Lol. But no matter, here I am, years later, still with a dream in my heart, and not only that, I choose to continue to pursue this dream, and nothing or no one, and nothing that anyone says can or will stop me. I'm an artist; *from the cradle to the grave.*

This isn't just a blog, this is my message and my letter to the *Dreamers*. No matter what, *keep dreaming*. No matter if you're in a relationship with a partner that doesn't support you or believe in you, or if you're single and no one is on your team or in your corner; *keep believing*. You need no ones approval or validation to live the dream that is in *your* heart. Because after all, only you and you alone can make it happen anyway, so you might as well believe in yourself in spite of what others say or think. It isn't *their* dream, it's *yours*.

Again, in the words of James Allen;

*The dreamers are the saviors of the world. As the visible world is sustained by the **invisible**, so men (and women), through all their trials and sins and sordid vocations, are nourished by the beautiful visions of their solitary dreamers. Humanity cannot forget its dreamers; it cannot let their ideas fade and die; it lives in them; it knows them as the realities which it shall one day see and know...composer, sculptor, painter, poet, prophet, sage, these are the makers of the afterworld, the architects of heaven. The world is beautiful because they have lived; without them all laboring humanity would perish....Dreams are the seedlings of realities.*

*Your circumstances may be uncongenial, but they shall not long remain so if you but perceive an Ideal and strive to reach it. You cannot travel **within** and stand still **without**.*

......The thoughtless, the ignorant, and the indolent.....they do not see the trials and failures and struggles which these men (and women) have voluntarily encountered....they have no knowledge of the sacrifices they have made, of the undaunted efforts they have put forth, of the faith they

exercised....they do not know the darkness and the heartaches....Cherish your visions; cherish you ideals; cherish the music that stirs in your heart, the beauty that forms in your mind, the loveliness that drapes your purest thoughts, for out of them will grow all delightful conditions.....Dream lofty dreams, and as you dream, so shall you become. Your Vision is the promise of what you shall one day be; your Ideal is the prophecy of what you shall at last unveil.

WOW, I'M OK; EMBRACING MY INTROVERSION

One day I was on my way home from a job interview in Southfield, a city in the Metro Detroit area. While driving through the construction zone on Northwestern Highway I reminded myself that I needed to stop at the Barnes & Nobles on Orchard Lake road. Recently I had read two books by Steven Pressfield- *The War of Art* and *Turning Pro*- and I was wanting to pick up a third called *Do The Work.* In addition, Barnes & Nobles is one of the few remaining book stores in my area and I've always found it rather refreshing to pay it an occasional visit. After all, it's a quiet, relaxing, and a comfortable venue for introverts like myself. Needless to say, I was informed that the book that brought me through the doors and into the sanctuary of written knowledge was not available. I gave the store employee a nod and expressed my appreciation for his help. As I turned in disappointment to walk away, a bright yellow shape shined in my peripherals like a beacon of light from the heavens, like a burning bush it called out my name. I responded and turned to focus my eyes upon it, and saw the yellow cover of a book. The title read, *Introvert Power; Why Your Inner Life is Your Hidden Strength by Laurie Helgoe, PhD.* **EUREKA!!** I believe in destiny, and that day I was destined to *enter* Barnes & Noble in search of *Do The Work,* but I was destined to *leave* with *Introvert Power.* Disappointment quickly evaporated as I floated toward the checkout line. Elated, I exited, went to my car, drove home and got to reading it right away.

For me to say that this book was not only enlightening but profoundly affirming would be a gross understatement. Laurie was able to articulate so many things I and other introverts experience in a very practical and informative fashion. Not only did she describe what it is to be an introvert, but also that it's very normal and that we introverts make up approximately 50 percent of the population. Throughout the book she addresses several important issues dealing with both introversion and extroversion; from our society's promotion of extroversion over introversion, the bias' against introversion, etc. Most importantly, she boldly clarifies that introversion is not a condition, illness, or a handicap, it's a personality type, and it's *awesome* to be an introvert!

Introvert Power was also a timely read for me as well. Although it's been years since I emerged from the agoraphobia fog, at times I've questioned if perhaps I'm missing out on *out there* and *with them.* Helgoe helps to reinforce that it's natural to question one's self, but more natural for the introvert to stay their course and stay true to who they are. So no, I am not missing anything *out there with them.* I'm satisfied and comfortable with who I am, an introvert. I no longer feel invisible, I'm no longer wanting attention, to be seen or heard, I actually shun attention. *Party this Saturday?* Oh that sounds nice, I'll be at home comfortably working on my book, but you go ahead and have a good time. Or; *The girls don't notice me? Who Cares.* Truth be told, I can't afford one at this stage of my life anyway, lol. Most importantly, I've been single for nearly two years and I don't miss the stress of a relationship and I'm in no hurry to rush back into one. I'm not ready to give up all of this peace, freedom, and time to myself. Quiet is a necessity for me. Less is more. More quiet, less interaction, and more inner action in every aspect of my life. Quiet is definitely super important in the artistic realm of my life. As a writer, artist, and illustrator I must have quiet. I must be alone with my own thoughts. My mind is like a crockpot that cooks quietly, simmering with thoughts and ideals. Ideals that need time to marinate and simmer slowly until they are robust and fully flavored. Then and only then will the vision be ready to be served.

Unapologetic

"Why look for excuses not to do certain people, places, or things? Sometimes no is as good as it gets....When the honest answer is no...Say it. It saves everybody a lot of time."

-Lonnie Hunter

One evening I had a conversation with my roommate Stephen. Stephen is a go with the flow type of guy. He enjoys the company of friends, going out on the town to bars, parties, festivals, anywhere that there's action to be found and good times to be had. From time to time he would extend the invitation to me to join in and go out, to which I politely declined. On this one particular evening I was explaining to him our differences. More or less it went something like you're a social butterfly and I'm just a plain old introverted kind of guy. As I was talking I could hear an apologetic tone in my voice, and I think Stephen heard it and picked up on it as well, and he responded by saying this:

"Hey, don't ever feel that there's anything wrong with that....the world needs a balance of all sorts of different people....I like meeting all types of people....I like the outgoing (extroverted) people and the more laid back (introverted) people....the world needs the variety....you can't have too much of one thing."

It was very refreshing to hear this from him. Later I thought about what he said and reflected not only on that but also on what I had said that triggered his honest response. Why should I feel apologetic about who I am? Why should I refer to myself as *just a plain old introverted kind of guy*? Perhaps, for such a good portion of my life, had I fallen victim to what Helgoe described as the *Extrovert Assumption*? I'll also refer to it as the *Extrovert Appeal*. In our western culture our media assumes extroversion, and appeals to it. Our culture is so extrovert oriented, in so many ways, from the music industry, movies, commercials, sitcoms and so-called reality shows, magazines, etc. It's extroversion on steroids. Even our public venues cater to everything extroverted. I have a friend named Jayme aka J Money that is an excellent singer. She is actively on the scene performing gigs at local bars and clubs. Occasionally I'll go out to see and watch her perform, it's a great excuse to get myself out of the house and out on the scene every once in a while. The one place that I've watched her at is a nice restaurant slash bar called Social House. Their social media plug is # BE SOCIAL @socialhouse. I couldn't help but be amused at this, seeing that each time I went I was alone and sat by myself, LOL. The only person I knew there was Jayme. How ironic, an introvert sitting by himself in a placed aptly named Social House.

In our culture being extroverted is the thing to be, the way to go. The subliminal messages that are 'bluetoothed' into the minds of millions twenty-four seven are very powerful and effective. They convey the message that if you look like this, act this, and dress like this, than you're on the right track. It's all a part of the *American Dream Package Deal*. If one is not careful, they can easily lose their way in this extrovert driven society and end up apologizing for being introverted as if there's something sadly wrong about it. As Helgoe described it in the chapter called *From Apology to Acceptance- and Beyond* by saying, *"I'm sorry I can't be a better extrovert."* I'm not going to be sorry anymore, that's some straight up *BS*. Like my friend said, the world needs the variety, and the truth is that we're all a part of the variety, the majority is an illusion.

THE FRESH INTROVERT

One of my favorite films from back in the day is one called Fresh. Written and directed by Boaz Yakin, the film tells the tale of a brilliant 12 year old introverted boy named Fresh. The young boy is entrapped by the streets and the underground world of drugs working as a runner for some of New York's biggest kingpins. A pivotal scene in this film was one that involved Fresh and his polar opposite and highly extroverted friend Chucky. Fresh was mature beyond his years, a man in a child's body, and Chucky was loud and rambunctious, a child trying to be a man too soon. Nonetheless, they were kids. In this particular scene the two friends take a walk to one Fresh's hideaways; Fresh in silence,

Chucky running his mouth the whole way there. When the two arrive at Fresh's 'spot', Chucky makes mention to Fresh how quiet it is there, but the quiet is no issue to Fresh, he prefers it. Chucky continues and further describes the spot as a lonesome place, but in the same breathe he explains that when he is at home amongst his loud and boisterous family he often feels as if he is all alone. Fresh then summed it up by explaining to Chucky that the more people that are around, the easier it is to feel lonely.

The writers did something very poetic with this scene, you see, it was the *Extrovert* who eloquently described the *Introvert* as well as himself, and it was the *Introvert* who eloquently put it all in a nutshell. Beautiful. I, as I'm sure many introverts and even some extroverts alike, have had this feeling on quite a few occasions and I came to that exact realization many years ago. The bigger the crowd became around me, the lonelier I felt.

Now just for fun, let's consider some other famous introverted characters from movies that have resonated with me over the years. I'll start with two characters that Matt Damon made famous, from his role as Will Hunting in Good Will Hunting to his role as Jason Bourne in The Bourne Trilogy. Will, the brilliant but yet troubled young man, who takes the long daily train ride to Harvard to work as a janitor, yet all the while he is in deep thought constantly solving complex mathematical problems and theorems. Yes he had his small group of buddies, but he very much delighted in his solitude. Very much in the same way I relish mine for developing my written works of poetry. Jason Bourne was an introverted soldier in search of his lost and stolen identity. He had been violently brainwashed and his name was changed from David Webb to Jason Bourne after he volunteered for the Treadstone program. In a way, isn't it eerily similar to the way our society tries to subliminally brainwash so many of us into being the way *they* want us to be? Through every commercial, film, article, magazine cover, etc. Be skinny, get buff and get a six pack, party it up, get rich, get *extroverted!* It's easy, subconsciously, for one's identity to get blurred, or even lost in the elaborate mirage created by our media driven society. How about Neo of The Matrix Trilogy, played by real life introvert Keanu Reeves. Always in deep thought in the midst of the huh-bub, and coming up with the "Ah-ha" moment, the *eureka* moment, the "oh wait a minute I have the answer".....moment. Janet Jackson, aside from playing the role of Justice, an introverted poet in mourning in John Singelton's 1993 classic Poetic Justice, she, her famous late brother Michael, and their mother Katherine, all real life introverts. How about Johnny Depp, Prince, JK Rowling, and even Michael Jordan? Yep, all introverts. Even when I look back at the athletes I admired when I was growing up, surprisingly I've found that they too, were all introverts. While at Auburn University, Bo Jackson's coaches had to force him to do post-game interviews because he was so painfully uncomfortable with being front and center. Barry Sanders was the most elusive running back in NFL history, not only on the field but off of it as well, as he often would run past reporters who tried to "tackle" him for a post-game interview. Both Bo and Barry also led quiet lives away from the field. These theatrical and real life introverts are what I'll call, the *Fresh Introverts*. I too, am a *Fresh Introvert*. I'm cool with my own unique swag, I'm intelligent, I'm unique, I'm fly, and I got skills to pay the bills.

47

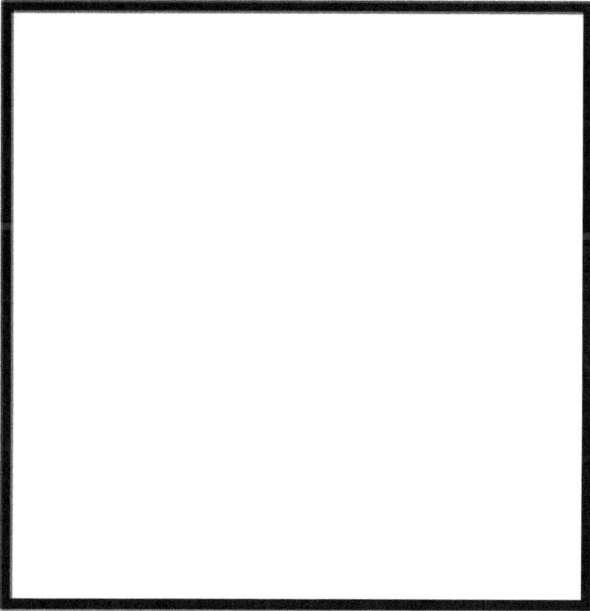

TAKE ME OUT!

Allow me to introduce myself;
People call me ID, your conscious mind.
Hi, I'm your Ego
I haven't been out for a while,
since like you were a teen or a child.
When's the last time we took a trip together?
When's the last time we broke bread together dogg?!!
C'mon n' feed me I'm freakin' starvin' dude!

Ooo, I'm missin' you,
dude tell me why the road turns?!!
I tried to reach you so many times
but you wouldn't lemme in?

Where are you man?!
Where am I in here?
All of this is so unfamiliar!
I don't recognize any of this!
I don't recognize any of you!
Do you even remember ME!
Do you think about ME!
You deposit fifty cents so I can throw in my 2,
since I gotta lot I gotta vent!
You got me bent!
It don't make any sense!
It ain't makin' any sense to ME!
You're no longer conscious of your own identity,
n' I've been cryin' out n' pleadin' relentlessly!
Can't you see you're meant for ME?!
You were sent to ME!
You need to just give in to ME!

Open up eyes so you can see all that we're meant to be!

How long will this masquerade last?
How long can you go on wearin' the same mask?
I'm sweatin' bullets in here I'm bout' to
faint cause I can't even gasp!
I gotta get sane, n' get the hell up outta this mask fast!
You need ME to evolve!
To keep you in order!
Evolution's the natural order,
but you've been cut down so much
that you lookin' a little shorter!
Shoulders hunched over dogg you look a little lower!
You regressed, walkin' round like you half dressed!
You don't even workout any more,
got man boobs on your chest!
You a hot mess, I guess
messin' with other side that got you possessed n' stressed!
They highlighted your weaknesses
n' then they burned all the rest!
They break you down!
I build you up!
They emptied you out!
I filled you up!
N' you throw ME out like yesterday's news?!
Dude wuts up?!!

You buried ME like the "N" word nigga!
N' you died slowly thereafter!
You forgot me on the altar,
n' now I'm just an ego altered,
you lemme go n' you n' ego faltered!!
Like a top haltered, you're only half a man

with only half to offer!
So you shouldn't be startled or alarmed
when Karma come back ta' harm ya',
cause you didn't listen to me n' all the people
who were for ya' n' tried ta' warn ya' n' inform ya',
there was a storm up ahead!
But you ignored us instead,
you ignored the alarm goin' off in ya' head,
you laid down with dogs n' fleas snug n' warm ya' bed!
You a discombobulated mess to me,
a foreigner n' I should call you Ted!
DUDE I JUST DON'T KNOW YOU ANYMORE!!!!
You need to take ME out so we can get reacquainted,
you gotta agree ya' life's a lot different without ME ain't it!
A lot less fun n' little bit tainted!!
Let's hook back up n' we can rearrange it!
Get it back on track n' change it!

You gotta lemme out so I can help you!
I'm the only friend you ever had who really felt you!
I kept you backbone straight n' your upper lip stiff,
your words were quick n' you never took crap from nobody!
I never let you take no junk or
get played like a chump or get punk'd!
Ego, never let you sink below sea level,
ME never let you hit the flo'!
But you went n' let me go now ya' lost like Nemo!
I'ma let you know like I told you befo'!
You need to take me out!

You don't talk to me or nothin'!
I'd love to partake in your midlife crisis but that'd be lame!
It's time to get up n' pep ya' step up n' step up yo' game!

You really can afford a little more of ME in your life...

Quit strokin' Mr. Pitiful,
That's a pitiful as can be,
I'm ya Ego come n' stroke ME!
I'm gettin' penis envy n' I don't like that junk!!!!
N' quit goin' down on Debi Downer,
chick got a dust cloud of misery around er',
n' pessimism surrounds er'!
She don't smile even when nobody's around er'!
She a ugly frowner!
But you let er' give you sloppy Joe head
n' you continue to pound er'!
Ooo, I wanna toss er' off a peer n' freakin' drown er'!
She got you meek n' weak,
Drainin' you from week to week!
Drainin' color from your cheeks!
Warm you up with fake grins
with crooked teeth to hide deceit!
You gotta dump that chick n' that chump change;
Be sure to get your receipt!
You need to hear me when I speak,
roll with ya' boy, you're only as good
as the company that you keep!

Forget those!
I can beat those, I'm your personal Jesus Ego,
your personal hero!
Holla at ya' boy!
Lemme be Pesci n' you can be Deniro!
Goodfellas!
C'mon let's do it for old time's sake!
We can defeat those!

But it's on you to take the 1st step!
You gotta take ME out!
I'm dyin' in here, break ME out!
I don't care what you gotta do to do it, just shake ME out!
I swear I'm bout' to lose it man you make ME shout!

You ain't lost, just undiscovered!
You possess boundless potential yet to be uncovered!
But we gotta work together, we need one another,
N' I really wanna help you, why wouldn't I?
You're like my brother!

Take some time n' meditate,
Check ya' head n' get it straight!
I see you got some kind of alias now, Emajinaysumthn!
Emajinay-man, emajinay-poet, well Emajinay-whatever!
Emajinay's-fine, but Emajinay-needs-to-mastermind,
You gotta follow yo' Emajinay-sign,
Emajinay-attarius!
Not a Libra or Aquarius!
This has gone too far dude we gotta start repairin' this
before it buries us!
You n' me against the world
n' together we can take care of this!
We gotta take care of US!

You've managed to maintain a healthy bond with
Your roommate name Procrastination,
slash/Nickname/Alias Constipation for the simple fact
that it's really hard to get any work out of em'!
N' frankly I don't like the way he's operatin';
He ain't a smooth operator!
He's a doppelgänger, opposite a stranger,

he don't offer nuthin' positive ta' change ya'!
You're the sum of my equation n' he's just n' odd remainder!
Let's add it up proper papa I gotta rearrange ya'!!
That's really what I came for,
To help you slip that noose before
it makes a knot ta' hang ya'!
I'm here to help you not to harm you,
I'm ya' Ego not a stranger!

What'll it take to make you believe?!
Make believe don't equate to BELIEVE!!
You gotta wipe the fog from ya' head n' take 2 Aleve!
To make you to see!
Let truth rake through ya' mind
like wind rakes through the trees,
Let it take you away like leaves take to a breeze!

You're under cerebral house arrest!
It's wise to be patient but foolish to be complacent,
Indolence is only another symptom of displacement, face it!
You gotta symptom diagnosed by Freud that you can't avoid!
I can't sit back quiet no more I'm makin' noise!
Get ME outta here! Take ME out!

DON'T BURST MY BUBBLE!!

Equipped with a gallon of
Willy Wonka's Magic Everlasting
Superextravaganzicunbustable
Wonder Bubble Formula #57
and my Hitchhiker's Guide to the Universe,
I step in n' outta my soap dish,

They tell me hope floats,
n' I hope I can float this;
I'm BUBBLE BOY!
The host minus the mostest!
Numero uno;
They say 1 is the loneliest!

BUBBLE BOY!
Bouncin' offa' clouds that I'm well up in,
Over rainbows in the bubble I'm enveloped in,
I stay up in here to keep the pain from developin',
N' it's cozy in here n' I think I'm gonna settle in!

Don't stand so close,
Watch ya' hands n' elbows;
Watch em' both!
Just stand back n' lemme float!
Don't burst my bubble this is my home,
don't burst my bubble just leave me alone!

Don't light up too close,
watch the flame n' watch the smoke...

Clip ya' fingernails n' try not to poke!
Don't burst my bubble,
Don't want hurt n' trouble,
just lemme float up high n' above you,
the only way you can see me is from the Hubble!
Look at the sky;
It's a bird, it's a plane, no it's a BUBBLE!!
Stay away, don't make me pop, n' fall into a puddle,
don't make me fall cause after all,
it took a lot of breath for me to blow up this bubble!

Weeble's Wobble but they don't fall down!
N' I'm ok with heights,
so I just wanna stay in here n' float all around!
I don't wanna let my ball hit the ground!

It's the way of this world ,
n' the weight of this world,
that makes me not even wanna STAY in this world,
another day in this world,
but no matter what I try I can't escape this world!
I'ma stay curled up in here, in await a new world!

I swear I feel outta place in this place,
so I like to float around in my own lil' space!
Float around to wherever the winds take,
n' it can blow hard enough to shake,
do whatever it wants, just as
long as my bubble doesn't break!

I'm too afraid to face my fears!
I can't take it here!
I was on a ship that wasn't s'posed to make it here!
I'm no relation to this world, I don't relate to here!
N' now I gotta a baby here,
this world is insane n' I gotta RAISE it here!
I really gotta get away from here!
It ain't safe out here!
So I'ma stay in here!
In my bubble, gotta make haste,
the chance I'll take,
to escape from here!

I ain't happy or elated here;

I'm disgruntled!
Thanks but NO THANKS!
To all the trouble,
n' that ain't me in a nutshell;
That's me in a BUBBLE!!

Agoraphobia, it was really nice knowin' ya'!
Eh, not really;
But a line of crap is really what I owe to ya'!
You n' the depression;
Forget the both of ya'!
I regret the day I got close to ya'!
Regret the day I spoke to ya'!
Hard to let go;
But it's time to break out n' be free like I'm supposed to;
Nah, check it out,
I'm gonna forget about everything I stress about,
I'm 'bout to let it out!
Remember everything I ever said about,
I'm settin' out to *gettin'* out,
Now lemme out!

The O^2 levels dropped,
CO^2's in my lungs like a clot!
Emergency evacuation!
Time's runnin' out on the clock!
Pulse racin' n' the bubble's droppin' like a rock!
Disoriented by vertigo n' I'm goin' into shock!
My arms flop!
I'm n' outta consciousness as I drop,
resistence is futile;
Ain't no way to make it stop,
yet I'm still screamin'; DON'T BURST MY… POP!!!

ODDBALL

I say and do things normal people don't say or do,
I'm not normal like other people and I'm not normal like you.
I'm not a freak I'm just unique.
I'm different and different is good.
And when the Lord made me
He made as different as He could.
Maybe I'm odd because I gotta be,
I'm an odd commodity,
consider me an oddity,
Cause I'm as odd as odd can be,
there's no one as odd as me,
I take normal tendencies and make
something called ten-oddecies,
and even to someone as odd as me,
I'm like the ODDBALL's Socrates,
intelligent but odd you see?
For no one is as odd as me,
being odd is more than life you see,
odd is like a job to me,
they don't make em' odd like me,
I'm on the oddest Odyssey.

I'm the originator of ODDOLOGY,
ain't nobody odd as me,
maybe a lot like me,
but not like me, cause;
I'm odd baby, yes I'm the oddest baby,
all these other odd suckas are just imitating,
Oddball Socrates.
With odd philosophies,
but ODD-ME is bout' clockin' G's,

cause I got a young girl to feed,
and I'm sure you know,
a kids got a lotta needs,
that's why on the streets it's hard to spot me,
cause I be on the clock all week,
and I hang by myself like an apostrophe,
I need a craniotomy to get the oddball outta me.

Shortly after birth I was aborted,
flushed down the toilet and deported,
to the land of misfit poets,
of course it left my world distorted,
I had no way to control it, now alone and unassorted,
devalued and unimportant.
Put out, type-cast as an outcast,
overlooked and bypassed, the crap happened that fast.
Went from a person with self-respect,
to an All-American reject.
It's not hard to detect,
I'm full of flaws and defects.
Hyphenated by silence,
abbreviated like an acronym,
constantly paused by commas,
a maelstrom of disarray between the quotations,
punctuated by a lack of self-preservation.
hangin' like an apostrophe,
life's become an atrocity,
It'll take a craniotomy to get the oddball outta me.

I know people look at me and
Say that I'm odd,
but nothin' they say or do,
can stop me from beating all the odds.

EveryBody's Favorite Screw Up

Say hello to everybody's favorite screw up!

Everybody think I'm *nothin'*,
I can't buy *nothin'*,
Provide *nothin'* n' I can't
get *nothin'* right,
There ain't *nothin'* I
can do right!
I'm a loser.
A low-life.
I'm a joke.
I'm irresponsible.
N' I inconvenience their lives!
So I'm pretty much worthless.
I ain't worth a dime or a cent,
I'm a penny with a whole in it,
I ain't *nothin*!

I've been evicted from my last three homes,
couldn't afford my rent,
lights n' gas, my car or my phone.
My money is funny,
Shit, I even owe my library money!

I've been messin' up for a minute,
and it feels like life ain't been fair,
all of these problems,
livin' at the bottom of the barrel
n' havin' nightmares @ the bottom.
'Can't-get-right', you say.
But it's just the way I am,

according to you, *right*?

So don't say hello to the *bad guy*,
say hello to the screw *up*!
But say hello for the last time,
cause look, I don't care what I look like to you,
I'm ready to change for *me*,
and do what I gotta do!

So say *goodnight* to the screw up,
cause it's the last time you're
gonna see me screw up like this again,
lemme tell ya'.

FAIR 4 A SQUARE

Yeah, circles are round n' smooth.
Yeah circles are cool.
But frankly I don't see what everybody has against squares.
Squares are multi-dimensional shapes with multiple sides,
that can be flipped in multiple
directions n' complex variations.
Ever solved a Rubix Cube dude?
If so, how long did it take?

See I'm fair for a square, rare for a square,
ain't nobody more fair, ain't nobody more square,
Square more, therefore why should I care more or care for,
people hate n' judge, don't care, that's what they're there for!
Therefore, I ain't 'bout to lose no hair,
cause on the contrare I'm pretty fair for a square!

L7's used to bein' overlooked by all the choosers,
step away cuz', my tables reserved for the losers!

So call me square but don't put me in a box!
Cause against popular opinion n' on the *contrare*,
I'm pretty fair for a square....

....I AIN'T LIKE NOBODY
HERE OR OVER THERE,
I'M DIFFERENT, I'M RARE!
N' I'M FAIR FOR A
SQUARE!

IncogEGO

IN-COG-NITO (INKÄG'NĒDŌ)
ADJECTIVE & ADVERB

1. HAVING ONE'S TRUE IDENTITY CONCEALED.

"IN ORDER TO OBSERVE YOU HAVE TO BE INCOGNITO"

SYNONYMS; UNDER AN ASSUMED NAME, UNDER A FALSE
NAME, IN DISGUISE, DISGUISED, UNDER COVER, IN
PLAIN CLOTHES, CAMOUFLAGED, UNIDENTIFIED.

E-GO (ĒGŌ)
NOUN

1. A PERSON'S SENSE OF SELF-ESTEEM OR SELF-
IMPORTANCE.

SYNONYMS; SELF-ESTEEM, SELF-IMPORTANCE, SELF-
WORTH, SELF-RESPECT, SELF-IMAGE, SELF-
CONFIDENCE.

PSYCHOANALYSIS- THE PART OF THE MIND THAT
MEDITATES BETWEEN THE CONSCIOUS AND
UNCONSCIOUS AND IS RESPONSIBLE FOR REALITY
TESTING AND A SENSE OF PERSONAL IDENTITY.

PHILOSOPHY- (IN METAPHYSICS) A CONSCIOUS THINKING
SUBJECT.

AGORAPHOBIA

My head, I think somebody's playin' games with it,
I gotta find a handicap spot & park my brain it.

Anxiety; it hides inside of me, hiding silently,
In a place that no one's eyes can see.

Wave by to me, say hi to me, at the same time to me....

Anxiety's right hand man is standing to the side of me,
Talkin junk n' jivin' me;

You live in private but I'm all up in ya privacy,
I don't care about propriety,
I hear all of your private pleas,
You wanna flee, don't lie to Me,
My friend you cannot hide from Me
I know the life you want is out there,
But I offer more variety.

My name's Agoraphobia, I got a hold a' ya,
n' I won't be letting go a' ya,
I got utter complete control a' ya!

Can't you see, I OWN you!!
YOU gave Me power....

N' now *I GOT YOU!!*

I've had you for years and days!
I got you livin' in fear n' feelin' some type of way!
ALL TYPES OF WAYS!!

I got you right where I want you,
Step outside if you're brave,
my voice'll haunt you and taunt you!
Yeah you're right where I want you, in my insane asylum,
All expenses paid, stay n' be as lame as I am,
Get a new identity, think of new names n' try em',
See I'da named ya somethin' else
but ya Mama named ya Brian!
No matter, I'm Agoraphobia, n' I got you agora *Phobic*,
Got you thinkin' n' feelin' like you ain't got NO sense!
I have you feelin' mental and livin' below your potential,
I keep you feelin' like dirt,
I make you question who you are
n' keep you doubting your worth,
You can't get nothin' right n' nothin' ever works,
I'm in up ya' butt like a hemorrhoid;
The more you push the more it hurts!!

I GOT YOU!!

I got you feelin' lonely;
No friends.
No woman.
No life.
Population 7 billion n' I got you just chillin' by ya' self,
Got a kid can't cop an occupation
to take care of ya' self,
Got you watchin' Christy Mack ejaculatin' on ya' self,
Got you lookin' at the ceiling
sleepin' in a basement by ya' self,
I got you sick n' got you
discombobulated n' beside ya' self,
Got you waitin', got you wastin',

try to sleep I keep you wide awake,
N' I got you enslaved to Me and I'm your obligation,
I got your brain intoxicated, you gotta be inoculated
to escape what I've created!
Wanna start a confrontation?
It's Me & You; mono e mono altercation!
I'll knock you out no hesitation!
I'm Agoraphobia!
I told you bruh'!
You couldn't defeat Me if you was
Obi Wan Kanobi bruh', n' Obi Wan can blow me bruh!!
Stay in here with me, there so much I can show ya bruh!!
The world is cold and callous
They'll judge you and mistreat you,
But I'll be right here; you *hear*?
When your palms are sweaty
n you can't breathe.
You hide it well but I can tell, inside you're just a mess,
I can feel your pulse rate and
your heart pounding in your chest!
Between this that an the stress,
No need for therapists; they thera-pests!
I can help you manage it the best,
I'll even cost you more but give you less,
Walk with me talk with me,
let your inner demons manifest.

I AM

I can protect you I AM Lord Frollo.
You're my little Hunchback in
my Notre Dame, Notre 'dame',

I manipulate you n' ignore your pain,
Wear your shame,
neglect your change,
I can give so much more,
But just more of the same.
I bring the pain, I'm as big as Bane,
I am a wolf in sheep's clothing,
I'll pull the wool over your eyes!
You're bright days will be dark nights,
You're my prisoner.
Institutionalized. Deeply initiated in the
League of Shadows.
Withdraw into the trees of shadows.
I'm a tree who's roots are shallow,
But I'm well grounded in You,
I hold the hammer & the stake and I pound it in you,
Straight through your heart,
straight through your dreams,
Pick you apart, leave you torn at the seams.
I am Old Faithful, I set off like clockwork!
I am forever faithful and deeply committed to ensuring
the preservation of your misery.
I am *misery* and you've been
good company for a long time.
Yes I am faithful to you.
Go to sleep I'm here, wake up I'm here,
I'm the man in ya' nightmares and
the man lookin' at you in the mirror.
I'm here to stay, I'm in it for the long run
and I'll never go away.
I am a parasite and you're my host,
N' I reside inside of you and possess you like a ghost.
I am everything I am nothing,

I am your problem and solution,
But most of all, I am simply nothing more than an *Illusion*.

IMMORTAL MAN

It cost me nuthin' to be born,
N' surely I won't be charged a cent to die,
It's living that costs me so much,
Or as Dickinson said,
"Life is the cost of death."
At times I feel that mortality sucks.
How much longer must I dwell on this Earth?
To dwell amongst misery n' hurt?
Sorrow n' strife, grief n' sadness?
How much longer must I endure my loneliness? *Madness!*
I believe in God n' trust that things do get better, eventually.
But sometimes I just wanna get the hell outta here.
I trust that life will be altogether different on the other side.
So much better.
I pray that when I arrive there,
I can shed this mortal shell,
Clothe myself in immortality n' start fresh.
That's the ultimate desire of the Creator Himself isn't it?
To start fresh? To start over?
To end this madness.
Redeem broken spirits n' banish all sadness?
At times, I long to be immortal.
I long to transcend it all.
O' how I envy an immortal.
Forever free of human inflictions n' sorrows,
Singin'……
No time to lend, no time to be borrowed,

We immortals don't stress over tomorrows.

I believe there's an equal amount of
Envy shared between the two.
I think immortals envy mortals
who acknowledge their mortality and
live each day to the fullest extent,
But they despise those who waste what little time
they **are** granted; N' take it for granted.
Lord knows I don't wanna do that.
Cause just to know that I was created
to experience something that God made
just for me to be a part of;
That's freakin' sweet! It's amazing!
To experience the good n' evil of everything
N' to mold it all, n' weave n' thread the needle,
N' tie it into the fabric n' intricately woven tapestry of
what we call the Human Experience.
Truly a beautiful thing,
So for whatever duration of time God has predestined
for me to endure it all, I must endure.
Endure. I. Mortal Man. I must endure.
Although times may try me
n' things from day to day may just
flat out freakin' suck!
I love life, I love bein' alive, n' I love bein' mortal.
N' I plan on enjoying my mortality for as long
As the good Lord allows.
N' I'm gonna play my part in an attempt
to extend my mortality as best as I can.
Like so, and it goes as follows;
For starters:
Honor my mother & father.

That ones easy.
Keep stress n' drama to a minimum,
Now what, oh yes,
Don't drive drunk or allow my friends to drive drunk.
Especially with *me* in the car!
Or, just don't drink. Period.
Stop smoking cigarettes.
I won't snort anything up my nostrils other than oxygen.
Crack kills n' stay away from needles.
Practice good eating habits n' exercise.
Avoid gun play and other life threatening altercations.
Don't mess with dangerous species of wildlife,
Look both ways before crossing the street.
ALWAYS use a rubber!
Even if she looks like *she's* never been
removed from a package!
Don't play with explosives or combustible chemicals!
Avoid goin' outside while wearin'
steel-toed boots in a lightning storm,
or playin' with the clock radio in the bathtub.
N' keep my neck out of strangulation devices.
I think that just about covers everything.
There's more but that's the gist of it.
You see, I'm gonna try my best
to extend my mortality as best as I can.
Cause life's too short n' there's just some junk
that ain't worth dyin' over!
N' I ain't in no hurry to be immortal.
Immortality can wait.
So however long it takes for the Lord
to call me up so that I can transcend,
Whenever that time is, I don't know.
That's in God's hands.

So till' then I'm just gonna live it out to the full.
N' endure.
Cause at the end of the day
I love life, I love bein' alive, n' I love bein' mortal.
N' that in a sense,
Makes me immortal already.
I am; an Immortal Man.

FACADA

It's a shame how people dress up in certain ways,
To appeal to certain people.

Wardrobes are so misleading,
N' many wear facades like wardrobes,
Coverin' up their true essence,
Seekin' respect, love, n' acceptance via vicarious methods...

Clothes n' facades conceal so much,
Clothes conceal the essence of nudity,
Facades conceal truth,
Both cloaking what lies beneath.

If not for facades we would know
exactly who it is were dealin' with
without jumpin' through loops.
Oh, he's a psychopath; Peace.
Oh, she's a pathological liar;
Ain't sharin' no information with you.
Damn, you got a lot of skeletons in yo' closet!
Need a shovel!
Wow, hold the phone;

There's actually a genuine, authentic life form;
A HUMAN BEING!
GOD BLESS YOU!
If it weren't for clothes n' facades,
or n' apple n' a serpent in the grass,
we could all truly see ourselves for
WHAT & WHO we TRULY are!
Without cause or reason to hide.
Anything.

Many rock the Rocawear, the PHAT FARM,
The Prada, Ed Hardy, NIKE, REEBOK, ADIDAS,
Levi Straus, Old Navy, or they shop at Gadzooks n' PacSun.
Everybody's clothed up in different brands
But the #1 brand a lot of people rock is that FACADA!
The oldest brand known to man.
Facada got more nostalgia than Lacoste
n' it's hotta than Prada,
Who needs Gucci or Louie?
Ooo-wee! Who's he!
You see in the new tee!
Breathe fresh, with style kickin' like Bruce Lee!
Ain't gotta be sophisticated or come off like a high roller,
But why rock Gucci when Facada can clothe us!

Dig this, Facada ain't legit,
N' I must admit,
That throughout my life I wore a few outfits!
For some friends I was with,
N' some girls I'd get,
Tryin' different arrangements,
Hopin' that they all would fit!
But I got lost n' split,

Cause I was forcin' it,
Pleasure turned to pain,
There was a cost in it!
I wore Facada for the people
wanting to see me being what I'm not,
N' couldn't love me for who I was or anything I that I got!
Apparels cover them scars n' embarrassin' tattoos,
That potbelly n' them saggy boobs,
My Facada did the same job, it covered whatever I'd choose,
I wore Facada hats, shirts, jeans, n' shoes,
in all different hues,
Like yellows n' reds you know; to cover up my blues.
Apparels I wear'll wear n' tear,
N' Facada kept me from feelin' bare,
N' I didn't care this is all that I'ma wear
n' strut around like Fred Astaire,
Until maybe there'll, be a day where I'll,
Start treatin' myself fair enough,
Take the time to care enough,
N' I won't need to keep wearin' stuff,
I played out n' I wear too much,
I'm wearin' up n' I'm tearin' up,
At the seams,
I need new jeans,
Brand new draws n' a shirt that's clean,
Pressed n' steamed,
No hand-me-downs I just wannabe ME!
Need a new wardrobe gotta change; I GOTTA!
Need new clothes cause' I'm tired of FACADA!

NO OPRAH FOR ME

I haven't written any
New York Bestsellers.

No self-help books that lead
to spiritual enlightenment.

I'm no fashion guru to the stars.

I'm no superstar gourmet chef;
I've never baked any life changing
cookies, cakes, or pies.

I've never starred in any
blockbuster motion pictures
or been on any hit TV series'.

I haven't been on Broadway.
No Oprah for Me.

No scientific breakthroughs,
No new male enhancement pills;
You can be rock hard without
The 40 Year Old Virgin side effect!!
I haven't developed any
revolutionizing make ups,
Anti-aging creams or hair products.
I haven't invented any
Gravity defying anti-boob sagging bras
for Victoria's Secret or anything!
No Oprah for Me.
No Favorite Things for Me.

I haven't saved any Humpback Whales
or opened any orphanages
in any third-world countries.
I haven't raised money to
build any villages.
I haven't adopted any children,
no I'm not the Octo-Dad!
I haven't contributed anything
to the education system.
I haven't saved any lives,
rescued people or animals from burning buildings.
No purple hearts or any medals of honor
of any kind have ever been issued in my name.
I'm just not that special I guess,
so no Oprah for me.
I'm a poet but let's face it;
I'm no Maya Angelou!!
MY GOD!!
WHAT WOULD IT TAKE?!!
My story's every bit of ordinary
and perhaps even every bit of boring.
Ain't nothin' tear jerkin'
or soul stirrin' or inspiring about Me!!
Oh no Oprah for Me.
No Favorite Things,
No trip to Australia,
No cruise ships,
No surprise visits from
any of my favorite celebrities!

I've never done anything
that this woman would
ever like or enjoy!

I'M NOT WORTHY!!

I REALLY don't have a chance!
Guess all I can do is
try my best to do good deeds.
Find ways to enrich my life
and the lives of those I love,
Live, love, n' learn,
and try to be the best person
that I know I can be.
All while reading my favorite books,
Watching my favorite shows,
Enjoying my favorite people,
and doing my favorite things.

QUESTIONS ONLY WHO CAN ANSWER?

You know I keep my dictionary n' my Bible side by side
or directly on top of one another on my bookshelf?
It's kinda symbolic, seeing as I'm constantly
tryin' to find the definition of it all,
N' what it all really means.
I won't take too much of your time,
but I just wonder sometimes…
Like God, if you're the universe
n' I'm made in your image, am I a universe?
Am I some sort of Micro Machines version of you?
Or are you actually smaller than all of this?
Like an Intel Pentium Processor operating the infinite plethora
of programs you've installed into existence?
N' everyone's always been under the assumption
that the universe is this great gargantuan

abyss that's forever expanding to no end.
But could it actually be something that's small enough
To fit on a flashdrive or an SD card?
Hell, man used to believe that the world was round, right?
Or better yet, could this all be like a dream
that's playing itself out in your mind?
N' if this universe is as infinite as you,
why would you create somethin' as small
as a human to exist in such a small world?
Cause I feel like I'm in a fishbowl sometimes!
This Earth's like a booger flicked
into the vast ocean of your universe,
n' I'm like a nose hair that just got stuck in it somehow!
That's crazy man!
Is there really light beneath the cosmos?
If so then where is it from n' what's it's purpose?
Is it the light of a projector casting the image of
this universe onto a cosmic screen?
Is it possible that it's projecting my yesterdays?
Are they replayin' in n' alternate universe?
Like somewhere on other side of a black hole or a star gate,
Replayin' themselves like episodes of The Days of Our Lives
like somethin' that someone recorded on a DVR?
Physicists have long acknowledged
that there are four dimensions,
Now there's data that may suggest the possibility
of seven others in addition to those four!
Do I exist in another dimension like Jet Li?
Does he look totally different?
Is he livin' n' feelin' totally different,
Is he livin' it up on my behalf?
My own personal intergalactic Avatar!
What would it feel like to operate with

100% of my brain's potential I wonder? LIMITLESS?
Probably a lot closer to "God" status huh?
Either that or I'd just be a human dynamo of sorts huh?
N' check it out, I know that biologist would refer to me as
Hominidae or homo sapien;
A creature with superior intelligence and articulate speech, or
the wise and knowing man, but what am I really?
Am I a constellation of DNA,
with stars connecting every portion of my skeletal frame,
n' I possess the ability to form any constellation I desire?
Or am I just a thought you thunk up?
That you think about for awhile, n' then I vanish the moment
you're tired of thinking of me?
I don't know, it's just somethin' I thought about.
N' why is my existence as the duration of a sunset?
Why am I payin' for the sin of another?
For somethin' I had nothin' to do with! (Or did I?)
I didn't eat from that tree! (Or did I?)
They say each is affected by the choices of another,
like links in a chain.
Are we linked through time n' space?
Are the 1st thoughts of time linked the ones I'm makin' now
and the 1st choices as well?
That'd mean that my choices have already been made, right?
As if I made the choice simultaneously with theirs
as if I would've made the same choice
that they did if I were in their shoes?
Even though they didn't wear shoes,
well actually they didn't wear anything!
But you know what I mean.

Do you have a counterpart?
Are you not God without the other half?

What we call that here on Earth is a soul mate,
one half that completes the other.
Who n' what completes you?
What's her name?
Is she nice?
Is she sweet?
Is she virtuous?
What type of stuff do y'all argue about?
She make you sleep in the other room
when she's ticked off at you,
or when she can't stand anymore of you snoring?
Does she not give you an....
Nah, I won't ask you that question!
How many children do the two of you have?
4, or maybe an additional 7?
How old are they n' what are their names?
Did you name one of them Heaven?
Are they similar to the universe that I live in?
Will it ever be possible that I could ever meet them?
Or maybe when I transcend will I be able to join the family?
You know somethin' dude, you're really quiet!
Other than a lot of nodding I really
haven't gotten much outta you!
But I'm sure there's good reason for it,
as there is for all other things, yeah?
Well I promised I wouldn't take up too much of your time so,
I'll be on my way n' I apologize if
at any time during this I sounded ridiculous,
But my inquiring mind gets a lil' squirrelly at times!
AHH, OH! You see that was a chuckle, I saw it *and* I heard it!
It's ok, you ain't gotta answer me right now,
we have all the time in the world.
But I was just wondering, you know?

ELABORATE ILLUSION

Time is fleeing like sand in the cupped
hands of children frolicking on the beach.
Time washes away with each tide
that kisses the shoreline,
whirlpools n' undertows
racking each grain & millisecond
into an eternal abyss.

I think to myself;
How can this ALL be real?

What's the ultimate purpose behind it all?
What is this universe?
This vast "something", this contraption,
This habitat, this seemingly endless thing?
Can it truly go on without end?
If not where does the end begin?
We often ask or wonder; Where are we?
The earth yes, but really,
Where is ALL of this?
Where does this really reside?
Where was it all manufactured?
Who's the architect who's mind is responsible for
this celestrial menagerie?
Who is this God?
This, Unmoved Mover, the 1st Mover?
And how could He or She have accomplished
a feat of such magnitude *so* well?!!
This world, this universe so well imagined,
so flawlessly engineered with incalculable precision,
all *so* real, yet all *so* impossible,

Completely unfathomable.
A dubious concoction of complicated simplicity.

In this elaborate illusion,
I can gather my conclusions,
n' still be wrong n' clueless,
Cause the thing about conclusions
is you can very seldom use em',
Take 2 thoughts n' fuse em' n' convoluté em',
But a bad connection'll confuse em'.

Born alone die alone
perhaps that's why I feel
like it's only ME.
Like it's been me all along.
Like everything n' everyone
else is an illusion
n' I'm the only thing that's real in this world.
N' that each individual is their own
world to themselves as well,
n' we'll each have
a world of our own to return to
when our time expires,
or when this illusion has
run it's course.

TEMPTATION

The desire for the forbidden…
is a captivating thing.

The trouble with resisting temptation
is it may never come again.

So should you reach that arm towards the sky,
Go ahead n' pluck that apple
From that branch,
Admire it n' take a bite?

Should you open that box?
Walk through the Field of Pandoras?
There's one with your name on it,
it plays a tune for you,
like a siren aloud it plays,
it plays for you.
The tune, the hum, the melody, that plays,
the bell that rings, the voice that sings;
Sings for you.

Go on n' put the key into that slot
and unleash the unknown.

Close the door in intuition's face,
turn a deaf ear to the still small voice;
The cautious whisper.
So ignore that label;
READ BEFORE OPENING.
Pay no mind to the contraindications,
the no return policy, no refund policy, final sale, as is.

No batteries or accessories included,
ignore the side effects,
neglect that little note from the Surgeon General.
Disregard the yellow tape;
PELIGRO.
CUIDADO.
Disregard that illegible fine print,
just signed on that dotted line thinkin' everything is fine,
That's what you think in your mind,
it's just a matter of time.
Till' it all unwinds.
Assume all liability....
For all that ensues.

MISPLACED

I set myself down somewhere
n' I haven't been able to find myself
for quite awhile now.

I could'a swore I was here,
or maybe I left ME over there,

If I can trace back my steps
I know I'll find ME somewhere.
Somehow.
Like if I find the exact position
of where I was standin' or sittin'
I'll get a Deja Vu or
perhaps a premonition!

The longer the search carries on

the more frantic I become.
I've already lost one
vital component of who I am,
n' in the search ta' rediscover ME
I'm inching closer to losing my *mind*.

I listen for the sound of my tell-tale heart
beating, thumping, laboring
within a dead man's chest,
near the point of failure
somewhere beneath the
boards of floors; a fading rhythm,
Fading to be heard; nevermore.
Alone upon a midnight dreary,
Beset and vexed not thinking clearly,
As before.
Above the door or beneath the floor,
Lost never to be found;
Nevermore?

O' so chilling the thought of ME
out there somewhere all alone
n' afraid in the dark and cold,
pleading for help.
Pleading for someone to come to my aid,
to rescue ME.
To find ME.
This is a search & rescue mission,
n' I have to lead the charge.

If I don't find ME,
all will be in ruins!
O' the whoa of being misplaced.

MISERY; MEET COMPANY

It's been kinda' difficult to measure myself these days.
Each day I lose myself in increments by the hour.
By the pints.
By the ounces.
By the liters.
I'm *so* stressed out!
My mind weighs in at 500 lbs,
My heart is a whopping 2 tons,
My soul is the weight of the water.
N' with each passing minute I can feel
every molecule of me being evaporated.
I'm eroding to the core.
The rigors of daily life take their toll,
Hitting me like cobble stones hurled by an angry mob.
When I awake to start each day
I only feel like three quarters of a man.
By mid-day I've already lost another 3rd of myself.
By the evening another quarter of me
has vanished into thin air.
N' when it's all said n' done
I'm even *less* than half the man I used to be!
Nothin' left to give,
Nothin' left to share with anyone else.
Do I have a significant other?
Well, if you mean anyone significant other than myself;
Than the answer is *no*.
Just numero uno solo lonely.
Everyday I feel like I'm just wasting;
Wasting away.
I must retreat to a place to waste away.
A place to drag my feet into,

A safe haven for Misery.
Perhaps I'll find someone there to share it with,
Someone who understands my woes,
Someone who understands my lil' Catch 22;
Understands how I can prefer to be alone
because being alone is when I'm most comfortable.
but also preferring to have a mind-set
that allows me to be comfortable amongst others
n' to be content with myself because being alone
can be just **downright**.... **aww** *FUHGETABOUTIT!*
I'm already here, ain't no sense in turnin' back now!

So I'll just sit here, n' try to make myself comfortable.
Sit here, dying a long, slow death,
to the tune of a sad song.
I can hear the violin, n' the pianist,
playing the soundtrack of my life.
My head slides to the rhythm of every
long drawn out note that's played,
and every key struck.
Play me a song,
I am a song that plays,
Play I some music.
Don't blare it, keep it soft n' mellow.
Yeah, right there.
Let it simmer, like n' idling flame.
N' pour me somethin' nice n' smooth,
somethin' cool n' bitter to drown these sorrows,
n' if you happen to be in the area come n' join me,
in this place where Misery meets Company.
Bring your heavy hearts and 5 o'clock shadows,
and slide a stool up to the bar
so we can enjoy a sad song

n' funnel our sorrows into our livers
till they harden in unison.
Liquor beatin' n' eatin' up livers like Prometheus!
Only to have it happen again the next day,
and the next day, and the next,
our livers re-grow over night but
vultures n' eagles don't go away!
They just stay!
They just hang around to play,
but that's ok, tonight's our night.
Let's enjoy our pity party!
Let's wash down the bitter taste of our woe 'till we overflow!
Pint by pint.
Ounce by ounce.
Liter by liter.
Just let it go!

We'll meet some new faces that we won't
remember the next day,
n' we'll bark at some floozy broads
till' we can no longer afford to pay,
n' walk away knowin' we ain't gettin' laid,
n' tomorrow we'll dial the fake
numbers that they passed our way.
Hey, whatta' ya' say!
Hell yeah, let the good times roll,
It'll never get old!
We'll prepare ourselves for the mornin' headache
n' the trip to the toilet bowl!
That's what's up!

Time really, really fly's when ya' life is stuck,
n' it's time to head out to paste myself to my loneliness again,

Cause my time is up, time to make my departure,
but before I drag myself to the parking lot,
n' stick my keys into someone else's car door,
I gotta bid ado to a few new partners;
I'm takin' off Sloth,
It's been nice talkin' with you,
n' Gluttony, it's been nice seein' you too,
before I bounce I'd like for you to meet these dudes,
let's gather for one last toast n' I'll introduce you;
Misery, meet Company and the rest of the crew.
Now ya'll enjoy yourselves n' maybe
I'll see you all here tomorrow evening.
But for now I must be on my way,
gotta get back home to crash out on my couch.
Lie down with my significant o-… *self*,
n' when I start my day tomorrow,
Maybe, just maybe;
I'll have a quarter left in my tank.

IDENTITY HUSTLE

I'm ain't dumb black n' lazy,
Drugged out thug'd out gun happy n' crazy,
I 8nt a spittin' image of how the media wants to portrait me,
I'm nothin' like the things they hear or that they say see;
Laid back, slang crack, uneducated!
But everyday thru my eyes all I saw was my struggle,
So I switched my lenses n' I focused on my hustle,
n' not even cause I wanted to,
But desperate times called for desperate measures,
'Specially when you got a lil' seed that loves you!
See I gotta make moves brotha',

Got bills to pay brotha'!
N' they don't run n' hide n' they don't run for cover!
They arrive on time n' pile up on one another!
I gotta stack cause I need that money,
that's gas in my tank,
n' more food in my tummy,
I 8nt tryin' to be bummy,
man I want somethin' yummy!
In a world where all they ever do is try to
take somethin' from me,
I don't have no other choice then to try n' get it honey!
Regardless of the climate,
Regardless of Uncle Sam,
I'm a hustler man n' I need a dolla for every gram,
If you don't like it then scram!
I had my swag up,
n' I was copin' up mad stuff,
my bills are paid so I don't really give a damn!
Look at me now loungin' in my pea coat,
See the time that I devote,
trappin' n' stackin' c-notes!

Gotta' watch where my money flow,
Gotta' know where it's flowin',
Gotta' watch it flow to see where it goes,
From where it came from n' to where it's goin',
So I can make sure it ain't a penny I'm blowin'!
Here, take this paper n' throw it in the cash box,
Keep it comin' n' keep it bubblin' like ham hocks!
Dudes on the block politic n' salute,
A lotta' hood rat chicks think that it's cute,
But I gotta hop in the coupe n' flyback to the coup,
To reboot n' regroup,

Re-up n' count up this new loot!

As I roll I hear a POOF!
Looked to my left n' saw a tiny version of myself
In an all red suit!
He had horns n' a pitchfork,
N' weighed me down like a boulder,
Then I turned to my right to look over,
N' I saw a mini-me with a halo restin' on my other shoulder!
Decked in all white; a stylish brother!
They cracked their knuckles,
Rolled their necks,
Then started beefin' with one another;

HALO: I won't sit back n' let you do what ur' doin'!

PITCHFORK: What you mean poindexter?
Ur' in this too n' I don't hear you complain
When the bills get paid by this E, Pluribus Unum!

HALO: You always say you gonna quit when ur'
in the mood n',
that won't be soon cause ur' steadily movin'!

PITCHFORK: Yeah, yeah, blah, blah,
What the hell are you provin'?
You had your chances but you took em' n' blew em!

HALO: Yeah, yeah, ha, ha,
I can't stand the crooked logic you usin',
you gotta adjust ya' attitude or go get a new one!

My Halo's tellin' me;

We can co-exist with one another,
can you hear me brother!
This lifestyle is gettin' you confused!
We need to find a way to match the Hustla' with the muse!
Find constructive avenues in which our talents can be used.
You're like dynamite at both ends but you runnin' outta fuse!
Where does that leave me?
B you gotta choose me!!

PITCHFORK: What, excuse me?
Listen here ya' big nose Dudley-Do-Good-lookin' punk!
Who you think you talkin' to!
You ain't no better than me!
Forget you!
I made you!
Punk I feed you!
You need **me**, I don't need **you**!

HALO: Hey B! Pay em' no mind,
Silence n' drown em' out!
Lemme put you on your feet n' tell you what it's all about;
You gonna make it my brotha',
Make it outta yo' lil' drought,
N' when it rains it'll pour;
You'll need a Ark to float you out!
Although your $ situation may at times be frightful,
A cold bed in a cell ain't so delightful,
You need to get your mind right n' start carin' bro'!
Cause this is all it takes lemme paint the scenario;
What you doin' kid n' where are ya' comin' n' goin' from?!
Said where ya' goin' kid n' what ya' got on ya' son?!
Who's the dude sellin' dope from outta his home to ya?!
N' what's the sellin' price n' what is it goin' for!

Tell the whole truth, the *whole*
truth we don't want no bologna!
Give us what we ask n' do whatever we want from ya'!
They got it out for ya' n' just like that, now they on ta' ya'!
Snitch spills, crib raided, marked bills, court cases,
Now you a goner bruh!
So so long to ya'!
As I ride I see it vividly,
Common sense is hittin' me,
Somethin' has gotten into me,
Hustle with my identity,
Relentlessly n' now it's really makin' sense to me;
I'm in too deep, n' people got it in for me!
But the truth of it all is I'm my own worst enemy!

Everyday livin' a lie.
Knowin' my hustle's the thing that
helps me sleep at night!
I can justify everything as long as the ends justify the means,
I mean, all things considered n' all things in between,
the bottom line was pesos n' cream
lining the pockets of my jeans,
But this ain't my callin' or what
Mom n' Poppa raised me to be,
I don't want em' both to one day see my face on TV,
like, is that my son?
No that is not HE,
Cause the character in jail's barriers
couldn't have came from we!
Seein' me in court waitin' for "your honor" to sentence me,
On my hands n' knees hopin' I can cop a plea,
But the state locks me up n' throws away the key!
N' as I'm taken away I offer everyone the same apology;

Dear Mama I'm sorry, you thought you knew me,
Daughter I'm sorry, you thought you knew me,
My lady I'm sorry, you thought you knew me,
Family n' friends, you all thought you knew me,
But what you thought you knew see
was misconstrued when you viewed me.
Yeah, this is somethin' that I vowed to never do.
N' the sad thing about it is;
Yeah, I thought I knew me too.

I'M A WRITER

Oral dictation was an original form of communication
and then it all flipped.
When people started communicatin' through dictation,
pictures and manuscript.
Everything comes from the mind of a writer.
From the builder man who makes things with his hands,
before he constructed it he had to write out his plans.
To the politician that's stands in the
lights of a public forum,
every speech he ever read he had a writer write it for em'.

See I'm a writer, it's what I do.
I write for me and I write for you too.
N' if you only knew,
some of the stuff I go through,
when I get stuck on a nice line and I can't flow through,
or find the right words to get my point through.
N' me n' Mary Jane broke up quite sometime ago
so I'm on my own when writer's block kicks in.
I just gotta sit back in wait for it to kick back in.

N' I can try and try, again and again,
when all of a sudden I'll be at work like;
"Hey! You gotta pen!?"

See TV n' movie productions come to
a screechin' halt without me!
TV & movie producers would be lost without me!
They beg for me to come off strike!
Cause I write like lightning strikes!

I write for my freedom,
to free myself from oppression, regression, and depression,
whenever I'm stressin' writin becomes my
contraception for protection.

I write feelings, write thoughts, write rhymes, write puns.
I write for pleasure and enjoyment, and I write for fun.

I can write me a right,
I can write me a wrong,
I write it right n' I never write it wrong,
I can right my life
when I write me a poem or a song,
I can write it short or I can write it long,
I write deep on life cause its what keeps me goin' on.
I write when it's right, I write when it's rough,
and at times I even feel like I don't write enough!

I write the news and share my worldly views,
and I don't work with signs it's the words I use,
I'm aligned with a muse, and at times I am amused
by the words I choose.

It's more than what I write or read,
It's what I drink it's what I eat,
It's what I feel, it's what I think,
It compels me to convert my consciousness into ink,
It breathes every time my chest heaves,
It dwells in my sleep n' dwells in my dreams,
Poetry is what my heart pumps when it's beats,
So when I'm cut or scratched poetry ink is what I leak,
Poetry isn't just a hobby,
But a necessity n' a need.
I am a writer best believe,
I am a writer yes indeed.

COMPLOVE

It all starts on a sheet.

On them, underneath & in between em'.

She lays down easy for me.

She gives herself to me.

She let's me have my way with her.
I turn her over, spiral-like,
Back n' forth she flips for me,
strokin' er' endlessly,
From margin to margin,
I make her spin tingle.

Our bond transcends
The physical realm.

She listens to me;
I can tell er' my story
n' share my life with her,
I can confide in her.
All the things I would never dare
share with another soul.
She deciphers my emotions,
No matter how trapped up
n' wrapped up I may be
in life's commotions,
She is my potion,
She helps me get open,
Whenever I'm low n' goin' cold,
n' low on hope n' I'm feelin' broken,
She offers atonement....

She reads between *my* lines,
O' to lay in her sheets;
My security blankets.
I release myself upon her and
she absorbs all of me.

MMM' I love paper!!

TORN

It began as a match made in heaven.
Since a wee lad,
A love so real, a love so true,
Ours was a colorful love,
An After School Special type of love,
Saturday Morning cartoons type of love,
A Crayola marker and colored pencil,
Type of love.

Throughout the day, together we'd lay,
We'd draw out our lives if I couldn't
go out and play.
Together as one mind,
We would conjure up worlds,
Then lay it all out, line for line.

But as I grew the pages turned.
I became infatuated
with a seductive siren.
Together we forged a relationship built on trust.
She was my post-high school sweetheart.
I didn't know what I was lookin' for in life,
I was lost and she came along,
She was there for me.
I mean, not that you weren't, she was just different,
You know?
She listened to me, she felt and understood me,
I mean, not that you didn't,
But I could just....spell it all out to her,
You know?
Ours was an As The World Turns and

a Wonder Years type of love,
A let it all out Poetic Justice,
Type of love.

Neither of us ever meant to hurt you,
but we have something special, something real.
N' I can't help or change the way I feel,
I'm torn in 2,
more drawn to her,
but more torn to you!
I wasn't born confused,
but I've always done whatever I was torn ta' do!
I desire to lie down in the same bed with the two of you,
lay each of you on a pillow to the right and left of me.
N' I, will nestle myself gently in
the space between you both.
Every man's fantasy fulfilled,
Ménage trois.

You have to understand that each of you are a gift to me,
gifts that I will never forget,
see I'll never forget you, never neglect you,
you've both helped me through
all the mess the world dishes out for me to get through.

For a long time I haven't been there for you,
to give you the attention you need,
n' the affection you truly deserve.

I know you're upset n' you wanna leave,
but I don't think I can let you,
and I don't think you really want to either.

I know I've failed to appreciate the beauty we've created,
but Baby don't leave me now;
we have children together, and more on the way.
Baby, I'll never desert you again,
give me another chance,
I'll paint a Monet Lisa tomorrow I swear!
The only writtin' I wish to do
at this moment is to *write* this wrong,
and we can write this love.
Ours will be a new type of love,
a Three's Company and Quiet Storm;
Type of love.
N' I'll spend the rest of my life fully devoted to you; *both*.
'Till the day I draw my last breath.

BEDTIME POETRY

It's 1-2-3-4, in the morning,
And I'm still up, tossin' and turnin' in my sheets,
Resistance is futile, this poem won't let me sleep.
I take poems to sleep with me,
They crawl between the sheets with me,
They snuggle up all next to me,
Yeah, that's how deep it goes,
We have a thing for one another,
In intimate relationship,
A love affair.
I pleasure myself with poetry.
I stroke my pen till' it ejaculates rhymes,
Let it splash all on the page till it formulates lines.

They're like lullabies.

OMG!! I gotta write this down,
It's reverberatin' in my soul so loud,
It's like a quake within me and
I feel it shake and I hear it pound!
That loud, distinct, distinguishable sound.
Of verbs, nouns, synonyms, and adjectives,
Twisting into metaphors & verbal optical illusions.

You see the pages keep on pilin' up!
Cause these emotions keep on risin' up!
So I gotta grab a pen and start writin' em' up!
Get on a mic and start recitin' em' up!
Poetry helps me find my loose screws and tightin' em' up!
N' when my mind is goin' through convulsions,
I use poetry to release my thoughts
n' all the stress I've been holdin',
this poetry acts as a potion,
when I'm goin' through a thang n'
goin' through the motions of commotions,
I can drown a drop of water n' a sea of my emotions,
n' a whirlpool positioned n the middle of the ocean.

I suffer from Poetic Insomnia,
I can't freakin' sleep,
shit I ain't even yawnin!
Ain't nothin on TV and the news is boring,
gotta get up at the crack of dawn n',
punch that time clock cause when bills rain it's pourin'!
1-2-3-4, I can't stop thinkin' so I write some more!

I don't set out to write on the thought provokin' tip,
I just write whatever provokes me to put it in manuscript.
N' I know I can turn a situation in a poem with no hesitation,

but the conundrum is;
Can I make a poem that can change a situation?
I guess that's the biggest "?" I'm facin',
but till then I'll just keep fillin' up the spaces of the pages.

1-2-3-4, I'm bout to have a cow,
my pen's upset and I just don't puke,
it's like projectile vomit now!
My bedtime poetry's like the 4th of July but even better,
when they shoot off in the sky
the fireworks explode with letters!
I see the cat in the cradle with a silver spoon,
Lil' Boy Blue & the Man in the Moon,
N' a witch came flyin' by on er' broom,
like I'm watchin' a Mazda commercial; ZOOM-ZOOM!!

The stuff that conjures up is off the wall,
swerves across the page like 3 retards
tryin' to drive a sweet car,
get in a wreck n' end up with 23 scars!

I paint pics with vivid imagery,
not just so you can feel it,
but so you can feel it vividly.

Been an artist from birth,
n' till' they lay me in my tomb,
If doctors X-Ray'd my Mama;
They'd find my art on the wall of er' womb!

See it comes from an inner source,
bedtime poetry intercourse,
it's when I like to play around,

I gotta write somethin' nice before I lay it down.
My pillow is a thought pad,
I wrap up in sheets of Mead when I lay in the bed!
I need some Propofol!
I haven't caught a wink n' a week, not a peep,
Lil' Bo Peep counted sheep to go to sleep,
but I count hooks, bars, n' stanzas!
My mind goes bananas like episodes of Bonanza!
Now I lay me down sleep,
I pray the Lord my pen to leak,
n' fill up sheets in between takin' leaks,
I pray the Lord my talents keep sweet,
Amen.

DREAM TEASE

You're so dirty,
You're so flirty,
Tell me I'm so perty,
then turn n' desert me,
O' how you burn me!
O' how you hurt me!
Truthfully speaking;
you really concern me!
I just wish you would take
time ta' learn me!
Put in the work n'
maybe you'll earn me!
You tell me I'm special,
you tell me you care,
you shouldn't tease me this way
I can give you everything baby,
whuddu'ya say?!!
You have no clue what
I can do for you!
I would never lie,
what I'm saying is true.

What do you fear?
The voices outside or the ones between your ears?

What do you fear?
The lies you've been told?
Is it failure?
Or the dragon guarding the gold?

What?!!

Are you afraid of me?!
Don't be afraid of what you say to ME!
I want you to wake up n' see!
Be brave n' BE,
all that you were made ta' BE!!
Take a chance and maybe we can fly away
n' find away to be free!!
Quite bein' a wuss, the chance you get
is the chance you take!
How long must I sit back n' wait?!!
How long must I carry all the weight?!!

If you let me go to waste then
it's just a wasted wait n' a heavy mistake
to take to Waste Management,
to decompose n' I don't think I can manage it.

You really doin a disservice to ya'self,
n' quit thinkin' the only one you hurtin' is ya'self,
selfish bastard; You hurtin' everybody else by
deserting ya' self,
rediscover ya' value an the worth in ya'self!
Take the time & make the time to work on ya'self!

Wake up!

Nothing comes to a
sleeper but a dream,
n' you've been dreamin' too long
It's time wake up!!!
Cause sleepers don't achieve!!

You fall asleep n' dream the 'Impossible Dream',

I want you know it ain't as impossible as it seems.
No matter what people have said, let em' say what they say!
Say you out of your mind! Even say you're a loser!
Loser? Who's the loser?!!
You the loser?
Oh no, it's them, the choosey choosers!
Who reneged on *their* choice,
Because they didn't choose it sooner!
People doubt you, make you turn and doubt yourself,
But they doubt you because
they doubt something about *their*-self,
They say you can't do that, and that it'll never happen,
Wish you good luck, and walk away laughing,
They told you to be practical, and only do the 'sure thing',
They can't see the beauty of *You*
cause they can't see what *you're* seeing!
They say to be realistic, and not to do what you feel,
But how can you be 'realistic' when you're unreal?

Freud said every person in your dreams is really *you*,
in your dreams you are everything and everybody too,
you're the Truth, so when you wake up everyday
you're a dream come true!
I'm just trying to make see that what I say is true….

.....AND TO REALIZE THAT
YOU ARE THE DREAM
THAT YOU NEED TO
WAKE UP TO!

ACKNOWLEDGEMENTS

STEVEN PRESSFIELD
The War of Art "Resistance: Defining the Enemy"
Black Irish Entertainment LLC, New York, NY, 2002,
Paperback Edition 2012
Mentioned in *Invisible: The Silent Gift*
with the permission of Steven Pressfield.

LAURIE HELGOE, PhD
Introvert Power: Why Your Inner Life is Your Hidden Strength
2nd Edition 2013
Sourcebooks, Naperville, IL
Introduction; Defining Our Terms pg.xxi,
The Fear of Solitude pg. 30
From Apology to Acceptance & Beyond pg. 224
All rights reserved. Used by permission.

JAMES ALLEN
As A Man Thinketh
Originally published 1902, Public Domain
Visions & Ideals
Effect of Thought on Circumstances pg. 10, pg. 13
The Thought Factor in Achievement pg. 36

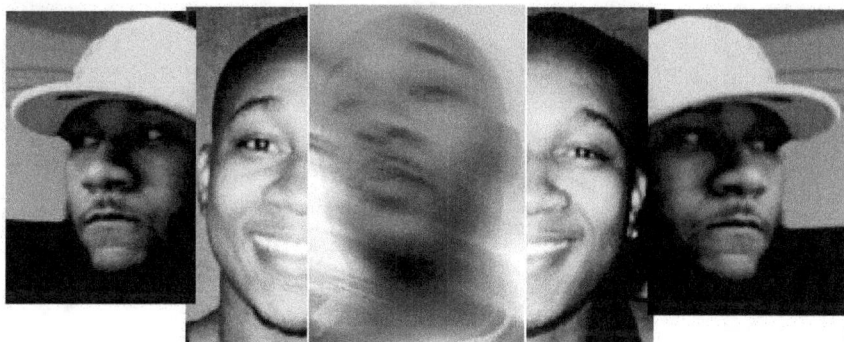

BRIAN HARPER, is a poet and artist. He was born in Detroit, Michigan and raised in Mentor, Ohio. He has been writing poetry for over fourteen years and this is his first published work as an author. He has worked as an entertainment writer for a webcast show called Actor's Reporter for Live Video, Inc.

www.ingramcontent.com/pod-product-compliance
Lightning Source LLC
LaVergne TN
LVHW052017080426
835513LV00018B/2065